What they say:

"There are a lot of capable bright people in the House of Representatives, and then there is Barney Frank. He has a keen intellect that intimidates many."
—*Rep. William Delahunt (D-MA)*

"He is usually the point guy on whatever we do."
—*Rep. Bill McCollum (R-FL)*

"One of the few congressmen who can draw a crowd of tourists to the galley over-looking the House floor."
—*George magazine*

"He fights! People are used to liberal wimps. Barney stands up to bullies."
—*Paul Begala, commentator & Democratic strategist*

"The blustery Newtonian is known in Congress for his ability to ad-lib a one-liner faster than he can light up a cigar."
—*The Boston Globe*

"I think Barney is being used as a surrogate for those too cowardly to debate me."
—*Ralph Nader*

"His witty sound bites are what have brought him the most attention—he kept his colleagues in the Massachusetts legislature in stitches."
—*The Boston Phoenix*

"Barney Frank—has become the Democrats' rhetorical standard-bearer in this time of defeat and confusion for his party."
—*The Nation*

"A pit bull of oratory and a star of C-Span."
—*New York Times Magazine*

"Frank has long been one of our favorite politicians in Washington, not only for his acerbic way with a sound bite but also because he has been a voice of reason on issues like military spending, the War on Drugs and gay rights."
—*Rolling Stone*

"The Congressman known in Washington as the left's attack dog for his devastating confrontations with the right."
—*The Progressive*

"Always an Attention-Getter—who does his homework."
—*Massachusetts Banker*

"In an era of buttoned-up, blow-dried moderation, Frank was and is a viscerally committed liberal: agile, acerbic and ferociously intelligent, the kind of Democrat who struck fear in the hearts of Republicans, conservatives and hypocrites of all ideological persuasions. His one-liners are legendary."
—*Newsweek*

"It is important to remember that for Barney Frank humor is a means to an end. Beneath the one-liners, he is a serious politician. Barney has always approached his job with a dedication that is common in civics books but rare in legislatures, and were it not for the fact that he clearly loves his work he would probably be labeled a workaholic."
—*City Limits*

"There aren't that many genuinely funny people in the world, and even fewer in politics. Barney is one of those few."
—*Jim Segel, former colleague*

"An enormously effective legislator, popular with his constituents and many of his peers in the House. He earned a reputation for his skills as an orator and is often referred to as the smartest man in Congress."
—*Playboy*

"One of the truly gifted legislators of our time."
—*The Almanac of American Politics*

"A master parliamentarian with a razor-sharp wit."
—*Boston Globe Magazine*

"Barney is a pit bull with a sense of humor, which is the most deadly combination you can have in politics."
—*Rep. Edward Markey (D-MA)*

"Barney Frank hates me."
—*Newt Gingrich, former Speaker of the House*

"Rep. Barney Frank has always been known for his smarts, as well as his wit and barbed speech—and Newt's nightmare."
—*Mother Jones*

"He holds arguably the safest seat in the House, where upper-middle-class liberals and working-class ethnics re-elect him routinely, often without opposition."
—*The New Republic*

"He's indispensable."
—*Rep. Jim McDermott (D-WA)*

Testimonials

Man of the Year
—*Americans for Democratic Action*

Best on Television
—*Washingtonian Magazine*

Congressman Rookie of the Year, 1982
—*U.S. News & World Report*

Dr. Martin Luther King, Jr. Distinguished Service Award
—*Bridgewater State College*

The Best Debater
—*Parade magazine*

One of the most influential House Members
—*Dossier*

One of the six best members of the House
—*Washington Monthly*

Among the Democrats' political and intellectual leaders
—*Congress Watch*

The Most Intelligent Member of the House of Representatives
—*Washingtonian poll of Capitol Staffers*

Recipient of the Order of Prince Henry Award
—*The government of Portugal*

Honorary Doctorate Degree
—*Southeastern Mass. University*

—Wheaton College
—Northeastern University
—New England School of Law
—Southern New England School of Law
—Bridgewater State College

Frank Talk

Frank Talk

◆

The Wit and Wisdom of **Barney Frank**

Edited & Compiled
By
Peter Bollen

iUniverse, Inc.
New York Lincoln Shanghai

Frank Talk
The Wit and Wisdom of Barney Frank

iUniverse books may be ordered through booksellers or by contacting:

iUniverse
2021 Pine Lake Road, Suite 100
Lincoln, NE 68512
www.iuniverse.com
1-800-Authors (1-800-288-4677)

Art work provided by:

Brian Woodson (c)
Eleanor Mill (c)
Dorothy Ahle (c)

First Edition

ISBN-13: 978-0-595-38117-3
ISBN-10: 0-595-38117-0

Printed in the United States of America

Contents

Biography

Congressman Frank graduated in 1962 from Harvard University. Subsequent to graduation he taught undergraduates at Harvard while studying for a Ph.D. Before completing his P.D. degree, Congressman Frank left graduate school to become the Chief Assistant to Mayor Kevin White of Boston.

After three years as Chief Assistant to Mayor White, in 1970 Congressman Frank spent six months as a fellow at the Institute of Politics at the John F. Kennedy School. He then served for one year as Administrative Assistant to Congressman Michael J. Harrington.

Om 1972 Congressman Frank was elected to the Massachusetts Legislature, where he served for eight years, until 1980. During that time, he entered Harvard Law School in September, 1974 and graduated in 1977. In 1979 he became a member of the Massachusetts Bar.

In 1980, Congressman Frank was elected to the United States House of Representatives where he continues to serve today. In his freshman year he was voted the outstanding freshman in a survey conducted by Public Television. In another evaluation of Congress, The Almanac of American Politics said "Frank is one of the intellectual and political leaders of the Democratic Party in the House, political theorist and pit bull at the same time." And, Politics in America noted "Frank's penchant for trying to match liberalism with hard-nosed pragmatism in order to move the legislative ball."

In Congress, Representative Frank is a member of the Judiciary Committee and the Banking Financial Services Committee.

Congressman Frank published a book in 1992 entitled Speaking Frankly, an essay on the role that the Democratic Party should play in the 1990s.

Congressman Frank has received honorary doctorates from a number of colleges and universities. Congressman Frank also taught part-time, while in state and local government, at the University of Massachusetts-Boston; the John F. Kennedy School at Harvard; and Boston University. He has published numerous essays on politics and public affairs.

Acknowledgments

I wish to thank the following individuals who, in various ways, assisted my efforts as well as supported me in piecing together this volume. Whether rendering opinions on reading the rough draft, submitting artwork and suggestions, the expertise of friends, family and colleagues all played an invaluable role. First and foremost, my wife, Ellen, was most patient with supporting this personal project and had confidence all along I'd pull this off. Certainly, Congressman Barney Frank supplied me (in content) with his constant wisdom and humor while performing his congressional duties and kept me on his mailing list, which I'm eternally grateful for.

As a sort of disclaimer, I should note that Congressman Frank once paid attention to a letter of complaint I sent out to various politicians which resulted in his role in overturning a piece of legislation in the House of Representatives. It impressed me that the congressman would not only pay attention to someone out of his district, but would personally take a principled action (successfully) to what he felt was an unfair issue. I was a devoted *Frankophile* even before the congressman heeded my concerns and it reinforced my regard for him that he acted on what we both felt was a bad piece of legislation. This volume is not a quid pro quo for Barney Frank's personal assistance (even if it were, I'd have no problem doing it), as I had been already collecting his many quotable bon mots for this eventual collection.

Thanks so much to my dad, Jim Bollen, another Barney fan and great humanitarian whose inspiration was unending. Also, to my late mother, Frances Bollen, who held the family together through thick and thin and complemented dad. Thanks to Bart Everly, the producer of the documentary, *Let's Get Frank*, who responded to my call and continues his good work in gaining support for his public showings of Barney Frank's important role in the Clinton Impeachment hearings. Also, many thanks to those whose opinions I value: Margaret Reimer, Melissa Norton, Dennis and Carmen Lone, David Plumer, Paul Hennessey,

Crush and Beedie Kean, George Bradt, Linda Impemba, Bill McNally, Frank Dodge, Ernie Ruest, Ellen & Paul Laincz, Perri Black along with Pam & Justin Ward of *Bridgton Books of Maine,* three of the most well-read folks I know, and to Jeff Crosby for his continued progressive activism which makes a difference. Thanks also to Steve Dosch from Barney Frank's office for his assistance. Thanks as well to cousin Jim Goodwin, publisher of *Red Eye Press* for his wisdom and continuing support of my projects. Special thanks to the following artists: Dorothy Ahle, Eleanor Mill, and Brian Woodson for permission to use their work in this volume. Heartfelt thanks to journalists—Claudia Dreifus, Joe Conason, Alex Beam and Dan Kennedy for their work and gracious support to use material from their work as well as *The New Republic* for selected passages. Honorable Mention and a big thank you to Richard and Kathy Cormier of *The Printery* in Bridgton Maine for their prompt and professional work with my project. And it goes without say that I'm grateful for my extended family—the Bollens, Plumers and Goodwins for their unconditional support of my projects. Blessings to all.

Author's Note

Why Barney Frank? This volume was inevitable. Essentially, this collection of witticisms, remarks, asides, pronunciations, exasperations and just plain straight talk is a book that wrote itself. Barney Frank is a walking, talking encyclopedia of quick wit, wisdom, and not a small notion of moral indignation to those values he holds dear.

This volume is an informal compilation of quotations by Congressman Frank from many sources. Many of Frank's quotations are memorable and are often repeated by those sources who've covered Frank's public career and have enjoyed his witty comments on a great range of topics.

As a popular interviewee because of his glib style, Frank has become a much requested personality on political talk shows over the years as well as a popular keynote speaker. Frank never disappoints whether he's railing against particular legislation, a political opponent or the general state of affairs. His ad-libs have become legendary. His command of the issues and strong point of view has made Congressman Frank a national figure and a respected leader of the Democratic party in the House of Representatives.

It is no accident that Barney Frank has been a popular incumbent in Massachusetts in the District he's represented for over 24 years. Actually, Frank has been "redistricted" two times in his career due to demographic changes. Recognized by his constituents as hard working and principled, Congressman Frank has been overwhelmingly reelected and several times without opposition. This collection of quotes by the outspoken congressman, is a testament to his unabashed straight-shooting along with his sharp wit and humor. Watching Barney Frank in action in the Halls of Congress is reminiscent of the fighting Progressive, Bob LaFollette with a touch of Groucho Marx. As his colleague, Rep. Edward Markey notes: "He's one of the few members who, when he takes to the floor, causes people all over the Capitol to turn up the volume on their TVs to see what he's saying. In almost every speech there's a line that will get to the heart of the argument."

An unabashed "Liberal" as he regards himself, Frank wears this label in a proud and traditional role as a public servant. Since his initial days as a Massachusetts state legislator to his career as a congressman, Barney Frank has built a following of admirers from the blue collar districts of New Bedford and Fall River to the upper class districts of Newton, Brookline and its surrounding area. Frank has built his career believing that government is there to serve people and to create a level playing field for those without a voice. Frank champions what he believes most voters want: a cleaner environment, safer workplaces, more government funding for health care and education, and economic fairness for workers, women, and minorities.

In his years in Congress, Frank has built a reputation as a respected leader on many fronts—as an expert debater of the issues; a master parliamentarian; a point man for his party on legislation and one who is unafraid to take on difficult issues such as gay rights or for legalizing the use of marijuana for medical purposes. Frank is a politician not poll driven but realistic in achieving his goals. Realizing that compromise is a given in the political system, Frank has criticized "ideological purists" for their uncompromising ways which have proven anathema for advancing certain causes. Historically, Frank explains that major social advances have been incremental and a pragmatic reality is often the way to realize certain goals.

Congressman Frank is an idealist and pragmatist and this has served him in his beliefs as a legislator. To best define this in his own words is as follows: "I reject the idea that pragmatism and idealism are opposed. The more idealistic you are, the more pragmatic you should be. The more you care about your values, the more you are morally obligated to get them implemented. It is not always easy to figure out how but you have to try: You try to reconcile your ideals and the real world." And further, Frank adds: "Unrealized ideals are not going to feed one poor kid. They don't advance the causes you're committed to. It's morally important to be as pragmatic as possible."

This compilation of quotations helps capture Barney Frank's motives—his values, humanity, sense of purpose as a public representative as well as his acute awareness of how the legislative process works and how he reacts to his perception of what's right and wrong in deciding various issues. Without apology, he evaluates the personalities involved in the major issues of the day—all, with the biting humor which has made him either a beloved figure by his admirers or an antagonist by his political opponents.

After over a quarter century in public service, Barney Frank's career has produced a treasure trove of commentary, ad-libs, barbs, and memorable phrases which help define a colorful career with a unique perspective of his world view.

The following quotations have been culled from interviews, congressional testimony, speeches, television, radio, press accounts, news releases and recollections by colleagues and reporters. It should be pointed out that the dates given at the end of each quote is either the actual year it was stated or *reported* in various media. Some were passed on through press accounts without a specific source date or have been paraphrased. As with historic wits such as Mark Twain, Oscar Wilde or even Yogi Berra, many of Frank's quotes have taken on a life of their own and have been used by writers, columnists and speakers.

For the aforementioned reasons, such a collection by definition has to be summed up as informal overall. Since Barney Frank often speaks extemporaneously, his quick quips must be recorded on the fly to be appreciated for posterity. Fortunately, being a public figure, Barney Frank's commentary is an open book to the public and there to provoke, educate, digest and certainly to entertain.

After two decades of covering the congressman's material in clippings, interviews, note-taking and research, it has been mostly a joy to amass this collection of wit & wisdom such as it is. It is hoped the reader finds it every bit as enjoyable as the enthusiasm put into it. It is also hoped that this collection enlightens and entertains as well as gives insight on how the political system functions from the acute eye of an exceptional public servant. As long as Barney Frank's public career thrives, we can be sure there will not be many dull moments—and we'll be richer for it.

1

Frank Talk: The Wit & Wisdom of Barney Frank

Political Opponents & Personalities

"There are rules of excessive civility around here to which I generally subscribe. You do need a certain amount of courtliness in the system. But that, in itself, can become a form of abuse. There are limits to when you restrain yourself from calling a fool a fool."

◆   ◆   ◆

"Unfortunately, because of absurd House rules which I am trying to change, comments that are critical of a Presidential administration or one of the political parties in Congress are sometimes barred from being mailed out to constituents, without extensive editing."

—2004

◆   ◆   ◆

While being questioned about an ethics bill which he co-sponsored, Frank commented about George H.W. Bush.

"I'm looking to the president-elect who said he would send us a bill. I've gotten better at reading his lips; I cannot read his mind. And so I will therefore have to wait and read his bill."

—1988

◆   ◆   ◆

When President-elect, George H.W. Bush stated that his priorities will be different from Ronald Reagan's, Frank responded:

"I think that is bizarre. The faithful George Bush who will not even tell us whether he whispered in Reagan's ear that selling arms to the Ayatollah was wrong all along secretly disagreed with Ronald Reagan on education. If you believe that, we have a bridge to sell."

—2000

◆   ◆   ◆

Frank shares his frustration with President Bush's appointment in an interview with *Inside Congressional Politics.*

"(H)e did appoint to administer the Civil Service—which deals with the non-discrimination in appointments—a woman that used to work for Pat Robertson, one of the great bigoted fools of our time."

—2002

◆　　◆　　◆

When Frank was in the Massachusetts legislature he had occasional bouts with Governor Michael Dukakis. The governor was known to take to riding to work on the MBTA. A reporter asked Frank if he objected to Dukakis riding the subway.

"No, I don't object that he rides the subway. I merely object that he gets off at the State House."

—1981

◆　　◆　　◆

Frank described Governor Dukakis as a reverse Houdini.

"Houdini has other people tie him up and then he got out of it. The governor ties himself up and then claims he can't do anything."

—1981

◆　　◆　　◆

"Talking to the governor is like talking to Mount Rushmore."

—1988

◆　　◆　　◆

On Governor Dukakis as a presidential candidate:

"It's plausible if he wants to go out and work for it, but I don't think he does. It doesn't happen by sitting back—the vice president does, but not the presidency."

—1986

◆   ◆   ◆

Frank was once asked by a reporter whether Boston City Councillors should be elected on an at-large basis which was during a controversial period in Boston politics.

"The question isn't whether they should be allowed to run at large, the question is whether they should be allowed to remain at large."

—1981

◆   ◆   ◆

When asked how the state of Massachusetts should pay for enormous cost overruns of the Big Dig construction in Boston, Frank took a jibe at the controversial manager of the project.

"By state taxes, or if [James] Kerasiotes opens a charm school and we get a share of the revenue. Which one do you think will work? And that was on the record."

—2000

◆   ◆   ◆

In an interview in the *New York Review of Books*, Frank gives an account of his political nemesis, former Speaker of the House, Newt Gingrich and others.

"He is the least substantive major political figure I've ever seen. When I think of Henry Hyde, I think of abortion. When I think of

Jack Kemp, I think of economic opportunity. When I think of most conservatives, something of content comes to mind. Even when I think of wacky [Bob] Dornan, I think of his military views. But Gingrich in 17 years has never got into substantive stuff. And frankly, Democrats are having trouble working with him because he just knows so little about issues."

—1995

◆ ◆ ◆

"I despise Gingrich because of the negative effect he has on American politics."

—1996

◆ ◆ ◆

"I think he's the thinnest-skinned character assassin I ever met...He specializes in the politics of personal destruction."

—1995

◆ ◆ ◆

A *Boston Globe* editorial commented on Speaker Gingrich's list of misstatements and in a followup letter Barney Frank gave his comments.

"Your catalogue of the dishonest statements made by Newt Gingrich in the editorial ("Cute Newt Gingrich"—Aug. 18) was telling but incomplete...By Gingrich's standards, as long as a charge is politically useful, it doesn't make much difference if it's true."

—1991

◆ ◆ ◆

"Newt Gingrich issuing rules of decorum is like Mike Tyson reissuing the Marquis of Queensbury rules."

—1998

◆ ◆ ◆

"Newt had one major advantage: the luxury of irrelevance, and he's lost it."

—1994

◆ ◆ ◆

"This is a really big favor."

Frank was asked to portray Newt Gingrich in a pre-debate practice session between House Democratic leader, Richard Gephardt and House Speaker, Gingrich.

—1996

◆ ◆ ◆

During the stormy days when Speaker Gingrich and President Clinton were at odds, a meeting was held between the two principals. Gingrich insisted that the meeting was friendly. Frank was skeptical.

"I don't think either one was under oath describing it."

—1995

◆   ◆   ◆

Frank has maintained that in Speaker Gingrich's *Contract With America,* he and fellow Republicans wanted to pose the popular term limit provision but were hoping and realizing it would not really pass.

"That is like a car salesman saying, 'I didn't make a contract to sell you a car, only to show you a car."

—1995

◆   ◆   ◆

"[Gingrich is] the most dangerous guy in American politics. He clearly decided he was going to get power by totally demonizing the opposition both as individuals and as advocates of positive government."

—1995

◆   ◆   ◆

"When Newt Gingrich was in the House he decided that the Republicans would never win as long as people thought the Democrats were decent people with whom the Republicans disagreed. He had to show that the opponents were corrupt and vicious and immoral and unpatriotic. And Gingrich began this whole notion of being personally denunciatory."

—2004

◆   ◆   ◆

In day one of Gingrich's new leadership as Speaker of the House, he and the Republicans abolished several committees, instituted term limits on the chairmen and eliminated hundreds of congressional jobs. In the new minority, Frank spoke out.

"When you are in the majority, you inevitably have to defend some dumb things. But in one day, you have been dumber than we were in two years."

—1995

◆   ◆   ◆

When *Esquire* magazine ran its annual "Women We Love" issue, Newt Gingrich turned down the chance to praise his lesbian half-sister. Barney Frank was asked to respond and did say that he and Gingrich had one thing in common.

"We both love his sister."

—1995

◆   ◆   ◆

When California congressman, Bob Dornan, sought to overturn a Presidential order banning discrimination against homosexuals seeking security clearances it began a personal battle between Dornan and Frank.

"That's pretty stupid, even by his standards."

—1995

◆   ◆   ◆

Under the Clinton Administration the issues of gays in the military caused a national furor in congress. Barney Frank was the most outspoken on these issues and pointed his finger at those who crossed his path. He was especially harsh on Senator Sam Nunn, a fellow Democrat from Georgia.

"Nunn's been an outstanding bigot. This man has shown very little zeal in his career, but he was astonishingly active when he was leading the charge against gays and lesbians in the military."

—1996

◆   ◆   ◆

Frank has been known to chastise both Democrats and Republicans. He chided Senator Bill Bradley for saying that neither political party was addressing people's concerns.

"I don't understand how Bradley can claim to believe in what he does and then find everybody equally morally wanting. I mean, Bradley's been a Democrat all these years. What was he, like, on Mars or Venus? What was he doing to change this?"

—1996

◆   ◆   ◆

"[Bradley] in a good mood is a worse campaigner than I am in a bad mood."

—2000

◆   ◆   ◆

The Whitewater scandal investigation headed by independent counsel, Kenneth Starr, gave Barney Frank, a leading and consistent critic of Starr, prominent status on the Democratic committee. Frank kept his constant needling of Starr during the hearings. Although the Whitewater probe couldn't indict the Clintons, there were other victims including a top advisor, Web Hubbell. Here's Frank's take on these hearings regarding Starr:

"A serial indicter of Web Hubbell."

—1998

◆   ◆   ◆

"[Starr's hearings are] an impeachment in search of a high crime."

—1999

◆   ◆   ◆

"Mr. Starr, reflecting his bias, follows the principal that if you don't have anything bad to say, don't say anything at all. But that ought not to be the cue for this committee."

—1998

◆   ◆   ◆

On the House Judiciary Committee investigating impeachment articles against President Clinton, Barney Frank was a point man defending the President against the charges feeling that a high crime was never committed. Frank accused the Republican majority of 'deliberate vagueness.' Frank felt strongly that a trumped up case was being made to impeach Clinton.

"They look at Kenneth Starr's three charges, and they say, 'Whoa, we can't defend these,' so they obfuscate and dress them up."

—1998

◆   ◆   ◆

"Ken Starr has not enough to get the president, so he's seeking to discredit him."

—1998

When Starr's investigation extended to the questioning of the Clinton Administration's policy of hiring homosexuals, Frank wanted to understand why this related to the President's original charges.

"What was he [Starr] thinking of? Not even a strained line of reasoning offers the slightest justification for him being questioned by your employees in this manner."

—1997

When the Starr investigation was finally completed, Frank summed it up.

"No one has investigated so much and come up with so little."

—1999

Congressman Frank speaking on the House floor about one of the proposed juvenile justice amendments:

"It says you can't show, to someone under 17, a narrative description of sexual activity. Umm, I guess Mr. Starr may be in trouble."

—1999

When President-elect George H.W. Bush's assistant, Andrew Card, was asked where Bush would cut spending on his proposed "flexible freeze", he responded—"somewhere." Frank shot back.

"Somewhere? Well that certainly is a firm statement of priorities...He is going to cut where? Somewhere? Somewhere over the rainbow."

—1988

On Bush's running mate, Dan Quayle, Frank had this to say:

"No one outside his immediate family thinks Dan Quayle is suited to be vice president."

—1988

"How about Dan Quayle going to go to George Bush and tell him he has a crackpot idea when Dan Quayle is George Bush's crackpot idea?"

—1988

"George Bush has a very difficult time expressing himself seriously to adults."

—1988

Upon debating a defense budget and learning of the spending levels, Frank accused the Bush administration of being out of touch.

"It indicates that the administration and the world are on totally different books here. Unfortunately, George Bush's policy seems to be

*motivated by a terrible fear of offending anyone. I think Miss Man-
ners is running foreign policy. Why did he veto the Chinese students
bill? He didn't want to offend the Chinese government. Why can't we
pull 100,000 troops out of Europe? We might upset the allies. He's
always worrying about upsetting someone else."*

—1990

◆   ◆   ◆

Barney Frank was the point man for defending President Bill Clinton
during impeachment hearings. Frank had a lot of gripes against the way
prosecutor Kenneth Starr conducted the hearings as well as his modes of
operation.

*"What you had here was an effort by the right wing in this country
to destroy a man [Clinton] whose political success was making them
almost crazy."*

—1999

◆   ◆   ◆

*"[The independent counselor] is on a crotch patrol for eight sorry
months."*

—1999

◆   ◆   ◆

In a local speech, Frank thought that he might be in danger of receiving a
subpoena from Starr since he mockingly referred to him as a hamburger.

"He has become delusional and is under the impression that he is a hamburger, the United States is the state of Texas...I think Ken Starr is acting like a piece of meat...rump of horse."

—1998

◆   ◆   ◆

At one of the hearings, Frank badgered Starr about when he knew that President Clinton played no role in the alleged White House office scandal. Starr asserted there was no "date certain." Frank countered: "how about a date ambiguous?"—which provoked bipartisan laughter in the crowded hearing room.

—1998

◆   ◆   ◆

Frank stated that Starr was using the power of the legal system to silence his critics and undermine the First Amendment right of free speech.

"People have a constitutional right in this country to spread information. The notion that a prosecutor can summon people to find out what information they are spreading about him [Starr] is appalling."

—1998

◆   ◆   ◆

Although Frank has been a defender of President Bill Clinton, he has also been pretty frank in his constructive criticism of the president's actions when he disagrees with him.

"He lies by being technically accurate. I wish he would stop it. I wish he would have learned that 'I didn't inhale,' No, I didn't do it by standing on one leg on Thursday,' is just not worthy of him and

everybody sees through it. He's not 14 anymore trying to outsmart the principal."

—1998

◆   ◆   ◆

"I am a little bit bemused by people denouncing [Clinton] for lying about private sex, because they denounced me for telling the truth about it."

—1998

◆   ◆   ◆

"I admire the president a lot. One of his problems is that he thinks he can talk his way out of anything." The New Republic (c)

—1995

◆   ◆   ◆

In a televised debate with candidate, Chuck Morse, Barney was visibly upset at his opponent's constant recanting of reported statements on his positions.

"He's become a serial untruth teller."

—2004

◆   ◆   ◆

Frank had this to say about a former state representative who kept sending out self-serving pamphlets keeping his name in the limelight:

"[John Gray] is the only human who has to worry about Dutch Elm disease."

—1988

◆   ◆   ◆

Barney Frank has also occasionally given the elbow to his allies as well. When Ben Gilman from New York introduced a foreign policy bill gutting foreign aid, Frank quipped:

"This wouldn't happen if Ben Gilman were still alive. Ben is with us in person. It's too bad he can't be here in spirit."

—1995

◆   ◆   ◆

When Frank was warned by a fellow representative that he was skating on thin ice by raising questions on Newt Gingrich's political action committee in a congressional session, Frank shot back:

"I would ask for an additional thirty seconds, since I yielded to Tonya Harding over there."

—1995

◆   ◆   ◆

When Presidential candidate, Bob Dole, was publicized giving back campaign donations to a Republican gay group, The Log Cabin Republicans, he characterized this as a misunderstanding to which Frank responded:

"Does this mean Dole is going to accept the money? No, he regrets that it happened. Well, I'm sure Mussolini, if we could ask him,

would regret World War II. I mean people often regret fiascos. But that doesn't mean that they have any change of heart, morally."

—1995

◆　　◆　　◆

When congressman, Dick Armey, the Republican Majority Leader from Texas, referred to Barney Frank as Barney "Fag," Frank had this to say:

"[I believe Armey] does not subscribe to this kind of talk, but it was in the back of his mind. And it reflects the behavior of some of the people he's been around—people in the conservative wing of the Republican Party, the cruder part of that party, who are angry at me."

—1995

◆　　◆　　◆

Congressman Dick Armey said he merely 'mispronounced' Frank's name.

"They've [my family] never heard anyone mispronounce our name that way. My mother told me that in the 59 years since she married my father, no one ever called her Elsie Fag.'"

—1995

◆　　◆　　◆

When Federal Reserve chairman, Alan Greenspan, endorsed the Bush tax cuts in 2001 and then three years later announced that the government could not afford to meet Social Security commitments, Frank pointed out the hypocrisy of his ways.

"Sometimes mixed metaphors say it best. Federal Reserve chairman Alan Greenspan's call for significant reductions in Social Security

can best be described as a case of the fox in the chicken coop crying wolf. He is greatly exaggerating the dimensions of a problem that he helped create."

—2004

◆　　　◆　　　◆

Another target for Frank is Moral Majority leader, Jerry Falwell, whose anti-gay pronouncements and bible-thumping have been a source of widespread publicity as well as political fodder used in campaigns.

"It's not just that Jerry Falwell is nutty, with his compulsion to be a public moron, attacking Teletubbies one week and the Antichrist the week before. But Americans now understand just how obsessive and mean this right wing is. They also understand that the right controls the Republicans."

—1999

◆　　　◆　　　◆

After Falwell attacked the PBS television Teletubbies show, Frank was asked to comment on it.

"In all fairness to Jerry Falwell, it's probably too sophisticated for him."

—1999

◆　　　◆　　　◆

When Frank's colleague, Rep. William Delahunt, attended some bipartisan breakfasts to work out a solution not to impeach President Clinton, Frank thought this was fruitless.

"I told Billy, the only thing you're gonna get from these breakfasts is cholesterol."

—1999

◆　　◆　　◆

During the impeachment hearings, Frank warned his fellow Democrats to let the Republicans continue their crusade in their revealing to the public scant regard for due process in taking down a popular president and the constant airing of tawdry details. Frank felt the public was tiring of these tactics as Clinton's popularity actually rose in the polls while impeachment was in the air.

"When your opponent is busy committing suicide, get out of his way."

—1999

◆　　◆　　◆

When the Supreme Court in 2003 struck down a Texas sodomy law as unconstitutional, Pennsylvania Senator, Rick Santorum predicted horrific personal acts were vindicated by this decision. Barney Frank was quick to answer this charge.

"This decision also casts further light on the stupidity of Senator Rick Santorum's assertion that any court decision which found that people's rights to private sexual activity was Constitutionally protected would inevitably lead that court to declare that bestiality, polygamy, and other sexual practices must also be condoned. Too often, people make bizarre predictions about the consequences of actions and aren't held to account when these consequences predictably fail to happen...I urge people in the media and elsewhere to subject Senator Santorum's bigotry to precisely this examination."

—2003

◆   ◆   ◆

Frank voted against a congressional resolution asking the television networks to withhold reporting the results of their exit polling until the California polls close in presidential elections.

"That's pandering to non-voters, as far as I'm concerned."

—1984

◆   ◆   ◆

During the 1984 presidential election, Frank was asked his opinion of candidate Gary Hart.

"He claims to be the leader of his generation. Well, I'm three or four years younger than he is, depending on which year he's using, and I must have been absent the day the vote was taken."

—1984

◆   ◆   ◆

During President Reagan's first term, Frank was asked his opinion of Ronald Reagan.

"Remarkably skillful at disassociating himself from his policies. Other politicians are jealous of him."

—1984

◆   ◆   ◆

In the aftermath of the attack on 9/11, MassPort authority security head, Joseph Lawless was relieved of his airport duties but acting governor, Jane

Swift, then kept him in charge of seaport security. Frank thought he understood the logic of this move by Swift.

> *"She was in the North End and she looked up at Old North Church and there was one light. You know what that means: They're coming by land. If she had seen two lights, she might have left him at the airport and not at the seaport."*

—2001

◆   ◆   ◆

When Frank spoke longer than his allocated time during a debate on term limits, he asked for two more minutes. The chairman gave him three more instead.

> *"My colleague from Massachusetts knows me better than I know myself."*

—1997

◆   ◆   ◆

Barney Frank was scheduled to receive the Excellence in Public Service Award for his work in housing for those with limited income. He refused to accept this award because of another party who was also awarded and which conflicted with his efforts.

> *"Precisely because my work with the Rental Housing Association is based on my goal of providing more and better housing for people of low and moderate income, I cannot agree to accept an award at a dinner which also honors Jerome Rappaport. I believe Mr. Rappaport's efforts over the many years have been highly deleterious to various efforts to provide affordable housing."*

—1993

◆   ◆   ◆

When commentator Robert Novak, on CNN TV, accused Frank of wanting a recession so that it would help Democrats, Frank responded to his charges.

"If you want to do cartoon shows, why don't you get one on Saturday mornings?"

—1986

◆   ◆   ◆

When Vermont Senator, James Jeffords, defected from the Republican party to become an Independent, Barney Frank gave his assessment of this defection.

"It is a measure of how reactionary Bush is that Jeffords could last eight years as a Republican with Reagan as president and couldn't last six months with Bush."

—2001

◆   ◆   ◆

Barney Frank has been known to turn down the occasional award or invitation when he feels they violate his sense of principles. Frank rejected an invitation to represent the Kennedy School of Government at Harvard's 350th Anniversary celebration in protest over an award given to U.S. Attorney General, Edwin Meese.

"From his attack on the Voters Rights Act early in this [Reagan] administration's first term, through his divisive and unneccessary effort to undo agreements to integrate police and fire departments...through his current efforts to appoint racists to the federal

bench, Mr. Meese has labored hard to undo racial progress we have made in this society at great pain in recent decades."

—1986

◆　　◆　　◆

Barney Frank cosponsored a letter urging Meese to step aside pending federal investigations into his conduct. The following is what he suspected would likely occur.

"If I were passing by the Republican cloak room and heard a cheer, my first guess would be that Ed Meese had just resigned."

—1988

◆　　◆　　◆

In an interview on a CNN television show, *Crossfire,* Frank responded to the comment that some of Attorney General Ed Meese's assistants chose to resign amid certain ethics charges against Meese. The comment was that 'the vultures have left.'

"What do you mean the vultures have left! The vultures just flew the coop."

—1988

◆　　◆　　◆

Frank often gives credit where credit is due. Here he comments on his political opponent, Rep. Dan Burton (R-IN), Chairman of the House Committee on Government Reform who's been outspoken in his scorn for liberal Democrats.

"Burton's willingness to take on the Bush administration has been impressive. His willingness to go after the memory of J. Edgar Hoover

is impressive. I thought his Clinton stuff was wacky. I'm critical of his positions. I'm less critical now of his motives."

—2002

◆　　　◆　　　◆

"Yes, I dislike Dan Burton. If he went back to doing some of the Clinton stuff, I'd be critical. But what goal is served by not encouraging him to go after these FBI abuses? Why would I not want to encourage that?"

—2002

◆　　　◆　　　◆

Frank occasionally responds to newspaper accounts which he feels reflect conflicting views of his. Here he responds in a letter criticizing a *Boston Globe* columnist.

"Of course op-ed pieces are for opinions, and balance is not required. But even by these permissive standards Dave Wilson's piece on ex-U.S. Rep. Paul Findley was so sharply biased that I felt like taking it to the gym and reading it on an incline board...His argument is generally unfettered by accuracy."

—1985

◆　　　◆　　　◆

Once again, Frank was compelled to respond to the columnist's charges in a followup letter to the *Boston Globe*.

"In his March 11 column about the proposed mall in South Attleboro, which we both support, David Wilson gratuitously suggested that I was somehow uncomfortable at being allied with 'a profit-motivated (yeccch!) shopping-mall developer (ugh!).' I would like to

make it clear that the phrases borrowed from MAD Magazine in that sentence are entirely Wilson's, and do not in any way reflect my views ('Tax revenue lost in the swamp'). The suggestion that I am somehow opposed in principle to the profit motive or to shopping-mall developers is, I assume, based on the stereotype that says that liberals are all secret collectivists. In my case—and in the case of most other liberals—the stereotype is an inaccurate one. Some of my best friends are shopping-mall developers, and nearly all of my friends are profit-motivated much of the time."

—1986

◆   ◆   ◆

When president-elect Ronald Reagan stopped by House Speaker, Tip O'Neill's office for a courtesy call, O'Neill showed him his desk which was originally chaired by former president, Grover Cleveland, to which Reagan replied: 'I played that guy in the movies.' Reagan was talking about Grover Cleveland Alexander, the great baseball pitcher he played in the film, *The Winning Team*. When Frank heard about this encounter he speculated on such a preposterous mix-up on Reagan's part.

"What could he possibly have been thinking? Did he figure that, after leaving the White House, old Grover went on to pitch a few seasons with the majors?"

—1987

◆   ◆   ◆

"Ronald Reagan believes in the free market like some people believe in unicorns."

—1987

◆   ◆   ◆

William Bennett was a controversial cabinet secretary under the Reagan Administration often giving his own ideas on personal morality. Frank commented on the publicity minded secretary.

"Don't stand between him and the camera. You'll get trampled."

—1987

◆   ◆   ◆

Frank commented on President Reagan's controversy of his work ethic where it was reported that he sometimes fell asleep during some Cabinet meetings.

"I don't begrudge Ronald Reagan an occasional nap. We must understand it's not the dozing off of Ronald Reagan that causes us problems. It's what he does on those moments when he's awake."

—1984

◆   ◆   ◆

"[J. Edgar Hoover is] an embodiment of most of the prejudices we've ever had. You have to take into account whether agents were slanting things for Hoover to make themselves look good."

—1996

◆   ◆   ◆

After the impeachment hearings, Frank was asked if he could still get along with his political opponents. Mostly, he felt he could work with them with some exceptions. Rep. Bob Barr, a Republican from Georgia was a notable exception.

"[M]y feeling has been that if Bob Barr caught on fire and I was holding a bucket of water, it would be a great act of discipline to pour it on him. I would do it, but I'd hate myself in the morning."

—1999

♦   ♦   ♦

Frank had this to say about the unfair criticism of Senator John Kerry over the years:

"He suffers from the fact that he's tall, good-looking, rich and articulate, and sometimes the resentment of his colleagues grows out of that."

—1985

♦   ♦   ♦

Frank had his assessment of another political opponent, Randall 'Duke' Cunningham (R-CA), noted for pointed and anti-gay remarks.

"He's not a guy who's taken all that seriously. He does not have a high reputation for the thoughtful, analytical content of his remarks."

—1998

♦   ♦   ♦

In a 1990 reelection campaign, Frank's new opponent, John Soto took an AIDS test and mailed the results to the media and then challenged Frank, being openly gay, to do the same. Frank was amused.

"[Soto] was so proud he passed a test he wanted to go public with it."

—1990

◆   ◆   ◆

Frank was asked about facing his new, and relatively unknown opponent, John Soto, about underestimating him in the campaign and if he posed a political threat, he couldn't resist a comment.

"It's a heavy responsibility to be all that stands between John Soto and reality, and I will discharge it to the best of my ability."

—1990

◆   ◆   ◆

When former Speaker of the House and fellow Massachusetts colleague, 'Tip' O'Neill retired, Frank's comments were heartfelt.

"The poor people will miss you and right wing won't."

—1986

◆   ◆   ◆

Frank, again responded to a newspaper columnist as he felt he was mis-represented in an article. Here, a *Boston Globe* columnist wrote a gossipy piece that the congressman objected to.

"Thanks to the fevered imagination of John Robinson, the Globe has a new accusation to lodge against elected officials, conspiracy to com-mit dinner…I have never understood why a serious newspaper like the Globe runs Robinson's column, which reads as it were written by a badly overdrawn caricature in a parody of a Dominick Dunne novel. But since you are a newspaper and not a novel, shouldn't you require him to keep his own fantasies under control and not allow him falsely to imply things which have no factual basis whatsoever?"

—1994

◆   ◆   ◆

At a congressional hearing, Attorney General Janet Reno described how she wished she had pumped sleeping gas into the Branch Davidian compound. Barney Frank was the questioner.

"Couldn't you pipe in C-Span?"

—1993

◆   ◆   ◆

Frank often has trouble suffering fools gladly and has been, from time to time, acerbic with what he feels are foolish questions. In a televised interview, a questioner was upset by the cast of presidential candidates and wondered how they got into office. Frank shot back:

"Do you think they were parachuted through windows?"

—1992

◆   ◆   ◆

Another comment from an official bureaucrat raised Frank's ire.

"At least one of the members of the MWRA ought to get a hackectomy for his comments."

—1991

◆   ◆   ◆

Former Republican candidate, Ray Shamie, from Massachusetts, was found to use a code name—'Fred'—when referring the John Birch Society. Frank couldn't help but be amused upon learning this.

"Now I know what Ray Shamie's campaign slogan should have been when he ran against Kennedy in 1982—Better Fred than Ted."

—**1984**

Neatness isn't everything.

Re-elect Barney

Barney Frank for State Representative

Barney will never cut a dashing figure. *But he has turned that to his advantage.*

ELEANOR MILL ILLUSTRATION

2

On Fundraising

One of Barney Frank's most endearing and entertaining qualities is his reaching out to his loyal supporters for campaign fundraising. The topics in his fundraising letters range from self deprecating humor; poetry; high comedy; a touch of literature and his own brand of verbal slapstick. In over 25 years of having to implore his supporters to help fund his campaigns, Frank has created a collection of letters that would make a worthy compilation in a league with *The Groucho Letters* or *The Letters of S.J. Perleman*. The following are selections from these letters:

> "*A funny thing happened to me on the way to defeat. I got re-elected. And I am finally writing to try to thank you for your part in providing the financial help which made it possible for me to confound the*

experts—myself among them—and win a race I was supposed to lose."

—1982

◆　　◆　　◆

"I realize the above sentence has a couple of words that aren't usually included in thank-yous. But having spent a good deal of my time (and your money) in the last two campaigns explaining things I'd said in earlier existences, I've become very careful about my use of words. I said "finally" because I realize that this expression of my gratitude comes very late. And I said "try" because I realize even more clearly that it is an inadequate expression of how deeply grateful I am."

—1982

◆　　◆　　◆

"I did try to be prompt in thanking those who were kind enough to contribute to me, but running my 1982 campaign, while still doing the job as a member of Congress in a substantially different district, overwhelmed me. I simply didn't have the resources to let you know more promptly how much I appreciated your help. Immediately after the election I was preoccupied—first by the need to collapse for about ten days; then by the need to arrange staff and offices for the new 70% of the district; and then by the lame duck session that never came alive but wouldn't die."

—1982

◆   ◆   ◆

"I have a Republican opponent and while he is not well known, he says he plans to run against my personality—which some people tell me is an issue on which I may be vulnerable. To be honest, I do not anticipate as difficult a campaign in 1984 as I had in 1980 or 1982—which is fortunate for my disposition and my waistline. But I am lobbied from time to time by former members of Congress who underestimated opponents and decided they had no need to campaign, and I am not eager to join their ranks. So, I intend to campaign actively and this requires among other things, money."

—1984

◆   ◆   ◆

"Since my need for dollars is greater than my instinct for modesty, I take pride when Politics in America says, '…he is also a serious, driven legislator, whose seats on four committees have allowed him to range over a variety of issues': or when American Politics says, 'He uses his impressive oratorical skills and rapid-fire wit to speak up and fight for those who don't have a voice in the political process.' I hope I won't be asking very often this year, but I also hope you can give generously soon so that I can plan a reasonable campaign. And I will, as in the past, be appreciative of any help you can give me."

—1984

◆   ◆   ◆

"Thank you for your campaign contribution. Because you and other friends have continued to be generous, I not only won re-election, I didn't get fat again…The response to my fundraising was more than sufficient to provide what I needed for a campaign appropriate to

this year's challenge, and I was thus able to win by a large margin—74%—and simultaneously keep my nerves, and thus my appetite in check."

—1984

◆   ◆   ◆

"I gain weight when I'm nervous, which I usually am during campaigns. Four years ago, I was nervous because I was afraid I wouldn't win. This time I had a pretty untough fight, so I started to get nervous that nobody else would be nervous and I wouldn't get the help I needed to run a good campaign and I would win by too little and have a tough fight again in 1986 and be nervous all over. One option was to pretend to be in jeopardy and send out the usual semi-hysterical appeals for a lot of money fast which candidates specialize in. But I didn't think it was wise or nice to try to mislead those of you who have been good to me, so I asked for some help while acknowledging that I needed it less than some others, thus fearing that by acknowledging that I didn't need a lot of help, I wouldn't get any at all."

—1984

◆   ◆   ◆

"I don't say as many things that you're not supposed to say as I used to, but I still think it's a good idea for politicians to talk like normal human beings part of the time, so here goes: it is unlikely that I will be defeated for re-election this year or in the foreseeable future. For someone whose temperament and physique react as badly to campaigns as mine, this is good news, but every silver lining has a cloud, and there is a down side to being relatively safe—I lose contact with friends who were so helpful to me when I had my tough campaigns of 1980 and 1982. You are used to hearing from me when I am in

desperate need of help. This time, I am writing not to ask for anything, but simply to report on my congressional activities, which your efforts have helped make possible."

—1986

"In my line of work, imitation isn't the sincerest form of flattery—denunciation is. For most of the past year I have been the target of a steady stream of misinformation, distortion, invention and inaccuracy. The ultra-right-wing Conservative Caucus has been among the most prominent of these attackers, joined by remnants of the Moral Majority, the Washington newspaper which is controlled by the Reverend Moon, and other random rightists. Obviously, what is flattering is not the content of their diatribes but the fact that they consider me to be enough of a threat to spend so much of their energy trying to diminish my effectiveness...I do need your financial support. I would very much appreciate whatever contribution you could make to my campaign."

—1990

"There are few things I dislike more than asking my friends for money, but one of them is not having enough of it to meet the needs of my campaign...My opponent makes wildly inaccurate charges against me on a regular basis. If he were a movie he would carry on his forehead a warning label: 'Any resemblance between this campaign and any fact living or dead is purely coincidental'...What this adds up to is that I have to ask you again if you can contribute to my campaign as you have in the past. Whatever you can or can't do now,

I want to repeat my appreciation of the help you have given in the past."

—1990

◆　　　◆　　　◆

"Some people told me when I first ran for Congress that the hardest part of the job would be fundraising. They were right, but not in the way that they meant. Asking for money is never fun, but I am lucky enough to have many generous and tolerant friends who make this easier than I had anticipated. The really hard part is trying to express, without being trite, the genuine gratitude I feel for people who have contributed to my political campaigns. Especially to those…who have stuck with me during the somewhat unconventional aspects of my career in the past few years, I will never be able to express my feelings adequately. You have made it possible for me to continue working at some of the things that are most important in my life, without having to make unfortunate compromises that the system in America sometimes demands."

—1991

◆　　　◆　　　◆

"I feel somewhat apologetic about what I am going to tell you: I do not plan to quit Congress. As I read the praise which the media lavishes on my colleagues who are retiring, I'm afraid my eagerness to keep working on a broad range of public policy issues may be taken as a character defect. So I hope that as character defects go, this one will be considered sufficiently minor for you to overlook…It is because you and others have been willing to contribute to me to advance our shared vision of what America can be that I have been able to keep this job and I am very grateful. Anything you can con-

tribute to help me with this year's effort will, of course, be similarly appreciated.

—1992

◆   ◆   ◆

"I know that good news-bad news jokes are trite. But campaign fundraising appeals from politicians are even triter, especially this time of year, so I have decided to do what those of us in politics often have to do and choose the lesser triteness. The news is that this is not a request for you to give me money. The bad news is that it is a request to give money to a larger cause—to a nationwide Democratic campaign which I believe offers us the best hope we have had in a long time for seeing the values that you and I share carried into public policy."

—1992

◆   ◆   ◆

"Writing a thank you note to campaign contributors in today's climate forces me to emulate Rube Goldberg without pictures. That is, I have to write something which reflects 1) my deep genuine gratitude on a personal level for your sending me a contribution to help me stay in Congress, counterbalanced by 2) my concern that someone reading this might infer something disparaging about our motives in engaging in the sinister process of "campaign finance", itself counterbalanced by 3) my interest in keeping you sufficiently happy with me—or insufficiently unhappy—so that you will continue to contribute, in turn counterbalanced by 4) my fear that the media will denounce me for accepting campaign contributions and therefore subjecting me to improper influence, albeit from proper people."

—1994

"I am reminded of the great line—from what you will not be surprised to learn is my favorite theatrical piece of all time—Fiorello. At the end of the first act, La Guardia celebrates his unexpected election as a Republican to Congress, over the expectations of those who had nominated him for what they thought was a safe Democratic seat, by turning to the bosses who nominated him and bellowing, 'I want you all to remember that my primary qualification for office is my monumental ingratitude.' I do not claim to be monumentally ungrateful, although I acknowledge that there are times when I am in a particularly grumpy mood when I may seem to be. But I do want to say that I am as appreciative as it is possible to be of your willingness to contribute to my campaign, based on our common belief in certain basic values, even as increasing public cynicism has tended to give this very generous practice a somewhat bad name."

—1994

"It's been a long time since I've written to my friends this much in advance of an election to ask for contributions—the last time was in 1983 when I had a debt to retire. But it's been an even longer time since I have felt that the values I came to Congress to fight for have been in as much jeopardy as I feel they are now...For example, in an article in the New Republic in February, writer Wes Kosova referred to me as "the most hated man in Gingrichdom." And there is a good deal of evidence that I am high up on the list of people the right wing wishes would go away. Speaker Gingrich, Majority Leader Armey, Rush Limbaugh, the National Review, Robert Novak, and a number of other leading right wing figures have singled me out for complaint, denunciation, or just plain insult within the last month. I do not cite all of this out of a sense of grievance. Indeed, given how vigorously I

oppose the things they want to do in terms of public policy, they are absolutely right to regard me as one of their opponents, and I'm flattered by their attention because it suggests that they think my opposition has been effective. But what is a boost to my ego early in 1995 could very well become a challenge to my career in 1996. That is, it seems to me unlikely that their unhappiness with me will remain purely rhetorical (as opposed to being rhetorically pure, which it certainly has not been.)"

—1995

◆   ◆   ◆

"Thank you very much for responding as you did to my most recent request for campaign funds...as I write this, I have just finished reading the USA Today squib about James Carville's referring to me as Barney Fife in his criticism of Richard Armey for having called me Barney Fag. Mr. Carville, who is a friend, explained that he obviously was thinking about the Andy Griffith Show when he referred to me in that way, and he contrasted what I make him think about with what Mr. Armey thinks about when I am the subject...so as I await the next variations of my name—Barney Google, Barney Rubble, or Barney the Dinosaur, depending on the generation of the speaker—it is nice to know that my friends remain my friends through it all. And as nearly as I and my campaign staff have been able to figure out, people have gotten my name right where it is most important—as the payee on the checks. For that I am very grateful, as of course I am for your continued willingness to provide the help that makes my career possible."

—1995

◆   ◆   ◆

"Fortunately, having been in electoral politics for 25 years, serving as a State Representative and then as a Member of the U.S. House of Representatives, I've had a good deal of experience in choosing the lesser evil. And that is what I am doing right now as I dictate this letter. Indeed, this letter is in fact the lesser evil in question—I am about as eager to write it as you are to read it. But writing it wins out over the greater evil which is to try to get reelected in 1998 without any campaign funds...To return to the point I was trying to make, it's an election year, I am running for reelection, and while I do not anticipate having to spend millions of dollars, I will have to spend more than I now have so if you think it is a good idea for me to be reelected, I hope you will send me some money."

—1998

◆   ◆   ◆

"I believe I am mellowing as I get older and am somewhat nicer than I used to be, but I concede that I am not yet at the point where I can win reelection on charm alone—which brings me to this letter, which in turn I hope brings you to send me some money."

—1998

◆   ◆   ◆

"In the interim between my writing to ask you for a contribution, and your very graciously sending one to me, the United States Senate killed campaign finance reform legislation for the year by filibustering it—more precisely, a 48 member minority of the Senate filibustered the bill, thwarting the efforts of a 52 member majority to pass it. According to the leaders of that filibuster, they were doing it in

*substantial part to protect your First Amendment rights to contrib-
ute to me. To them, legislation which restricts the role of vast
amounts of money in deciding electoral outcomes interferes with the
fundamental rights of the people in a democracy to express themselves. And merging that logic with a little Tom Sawyer-you-can
paint-my-fence logic, I suppose I should not be thanking you in this
letter, but expressing my gratification that I was able to do you the
service of being the vehicle by which you could exercise your First
Amendment right to send me money."*

—1998

◆   ◆   ◆

*"[Since] I was a supporter of the legislation which was filibustered
to death, I am probably not entitled to that set of logical jumps, so I
am writing this instead to express my profound appreciation to you
for sending me that contribution, and enabling me to both keep
enough money on hand to do what I have to do for reelection, and,
equally important, to do that in a way that keeps me clear of the kind
of fundraising that gets some of my colleagues in trouble...Inciden-
tally, I finally remembered where that meandering sentence was
going, and I can tell you that it was such a convoluted thought that
my ending the sentence in the fashion that I did was a literary mercy
killing."*

—1998

◆   ◆   ◆

Frank has from time to time, sent his supporters fundraising appeals to
consider donating to related causes and candidates who share the same philosophy and values as he does. As a successful fundraiser and serving in a relatively safe district, Frank has been generous and successful in helping
others. Here is an appeal for the *Americans for Democratic Action.*

"I am proud that in my career in politics I have managed to avoid one of our profession's most common failings—the practice of sending out wildly hyperbolic fundraising letters. So, I hope when I tell you that a contribution to ADA represents one of the most effective things you can do to advance the cause of liberalism at this critical political moment, you'll take it at face value and not subject it to the usual discounting that sensible people apply to political solicitations."

—2001

◆　　　◆　　　◆

"Since after nearly twenty years of begging, I am out of new ways to frame a logical argument for you to send me money, I equal them in need for a logical substitute. And since the fact that you are receiving this means that you have previously donated to my campaign, one particular quotation is especially appropriate: 'Please sir, I want some more.'*

*I apologize for addressing this to the considerable number of my contributors who are not 'sirs.' In the book, Oliver Twist was addressing a particular person who happened to be a man, and I have simply adopted a figure of speech in borrowing this comment addressed to a single person for use as a generalized request to thousands. My dim recollection from high school days is that there is a name for the figure of speech that allows a single comment to stand in a broader context, but I am uncertain as to what it is. I know it is not onomatopoeia, and it may or may not be synecdoche."

—1999

◆　　　◆　　　◆

"As I watched Strom Thurmond open the Senate impeachment trial of President Clinton, my thoughts explicably turned to the topic of setting some guideposts for myself to make sure that, the voters being

willing, I am not tempted to stay here longer than is reasonable, or at least tasteful. And I have come up with one good indicator that people in my line of work ought to use for deciding when to quit: at that point when you become demonstrably better at asking for money than at thanking people for sending it…I cannot think of a worse way to make a living than to be an elected official who feels unable to vote his or her conscience on important moral issues because of the fear that he or she will lose either votes or money. And I cannot think of a better way for me to live my professional life than to be able to do my job with the kind of freedom I have—thanks in part to you. My gratitude for this is complete."

—1999

"One of the things that I have thought about doing in retirement is compiling a list of sayings that are not remotely true. The idea of doing that recurred recently when I was inaccurately quoted in a newspaper in regard to something terrible that had happened as saying 'whatever doesn't kill us makes us stronger.' This is, of course, preposterous. The list of non-fatal events that leave us weaker is an enormous one. In case you are wondering, the relevance of this project to this letter is that among the things that people often say and rarely believe is that it is 'more blessed to give than to receive.' If that were in fact true, I would not be now trying to think of yet another new way to say thank you for the campaign donation you have given me. Instead, I would be sitting here awaiting thank you letters which would be owed to me if in fact giving was such a wonderful experience. After all, without a receiver, there can be no donor. However, (I have a nagging feeling that there is a rule which I have just broken against starting a sentence with however. Sorry…I will forebear easing my conscience by the thought that I have helped you by receiving your money on the theory that whatever

makes you poorer makes you richer—which makes as much sense as some of these other old sayings.)"

—2001

◆　　◆　　◆

"Over the years I have fallen into a pattern in the fundraising letters I send. Because my electoral situation at home has not been precarious, I have not hit the panic button and begged you to send me large amounts of money. And, because I am still deeply grateful to those who respond to my appeals, and seek ways to express this gratitude without the quid pro quo that can lead to bad newspaper stories at best and indictments at worst, I work hard on these letters in the hope that some modest entertainment value will show my appreciation…Having said that I would cut down on jokes, I will now violate that pledge. (Although I can say in defense of my consistency that it is a very old joke and not terribly funny.) The story is of a person who is asked to evaluate a restaurant and replies that the service is very bad but on the other hand you don't mind waiting because the food isn't very good when it comes. This employs the humorous device of reversing the point you expect to be made. That is, where you expect the second part of the argument to be compensatory, it instead reinforces the original point in an incongruous way. The relevance is that unlike my past letters in which I have tried to be very entertaining while asking you for only a little money, this letter will be much less entertaining, in return for which I hope you will send me more."

—2001

◆　　◆　　◆

"…I am asking you to contribute what you can to my campaign both to strengthen me for a more vigorous effort that I will be required to make next year, and help me contribute to others who share the val-

ues for which I have stood in my career. And if all this works out well, I promise you that in 2003, I will send you a hilarious letter very cheaply."

—2001

"According to fundraising professionals, fundraising letters generally do better when they are woeful. That is, people who get paid to tell other people how to get you to make a contribution believe that lamentation, worry and lurking disaster sell better than good cheer. Unfortunately for you, you are someone who tends to support causes and so your mail tends to be gloomier than most. Unfortunately for me, I seem to be running out of gloom. This doesn't mean that I think all is wonderful in our country and around the world. What it means is that unlike many of my friends and political allies (overlapping but hardly identical categories) I am optimistic about achieving important political goals…I ask for funds so that we can participate in an effort about which I am increasingly confident—focusing the enormous creative energies of this country on some of the most pressing domestic tasks we have too long ignored. (Of course, if this is not a good enough reason for me to come asking, I can always go back to gloom and doom next time.)"

—1991

"The efficient folks at Social Security reminded me that with my 62 nd birthday coming this month, I'm eligible for early retirement. But then I went onto the House floor and saw some of the people for whom my retirement would be a great gift, which reminded me of why I very much want to stay here. So I will be running for re-election, which means that in lieu of Social Security checks, I am solicit-

ing one from you. (This is as close as I will ever come to supporting any form of Social Security privatization.) I do not anticipate a tough re-election contest, but some opposition is likely, and I'm not quite at the point where I can win entirely on my charm...So I solicit you again—for the 25 th or 30 th time for some of you, whose continued willingness even to open mail from me leaves me genuinely abashed. I promise in return to make those politicians with whom you most strongly disagree, sorry that you did."

—2002

◆   ◆   ◆

"A couple of months ago I told you I wouldn't be asking for money unless I needed it. Well, I need it—at least some of it. I don't face major competition for re-election, and so I don't have to raise the kind of money that you've helped me raise in previous years. But I'm afraid I'm not going to be able to get by with no expenditures this year."

—1986

◆   ◆   ◆

"I have run out of prose with which to thank you for your contribution, so I will turn to poetry after which those of you who read this may turn against poetry—but it is the best I can do after twenty two years of thanking. By way of preface, I should point out that my district is a very diverse one and I do not think that any one form of poetry would appeal sufficiently to the full range of those who have supported me. I have therefore decided to employ two forms—a limerick and a haiku—each of which has the enormous virtue of being a hell of a lot shorter than a sonnet!"

I. *There once was a Congressman from Newton*
    Whose friends kindly sent lots of loot in.
    So when the right-wingers

Assailed him with zingers,
his own horn he could afford to be tootin'.
II. Congressman B. Frank
asked his friends to send money
and was glad they did.

—2002

◆   ◆   ◆

"Among the things that politicians say more often than they mean is that we regret not being able to talk to people face to face. Sometimes the impersonality of the printed page is a blessing. It is much easier to beg by letter than in person, and this impersonality is especially important to me on those occasions when I borrow from a song to help my schnorring. Singing is not one of the 2,477 things I do best. (This began to dawn on me in the second grade when Mrs. Doyle told me simply to move my lips while the rest of the class sang 'My Old Kentucky Home'. Replaying that in my mind a few years ago, I realized for the first time how blatantly racist the song is. The line 'it's summer and the darkies are gay' could be the theme for an especially tasteless Saturday Night Live sketch.) So it is because I am writing this to you rather than singing it, that I am able to fall back on one of the literary devices I have from time to time employed in my desperate effort not to say pretty much the same thing every time I hold my candidate's tin cup.*

'Will you still need me, will you still feed me, when I'm sixty-four?'

This letter will be arriving at your mailbox pretty close to March 31 st , which is my sixty-fourth birthday. (Actually, this may be a real instance of when there is some variation in what the meaning of is is—that is, for some of you by the time you get this, it would have been more accurate to say that March 31 st was my 64 th birthday. I apologize a little bit for this diversion, but isn't it nice to be brought back to the time when the only dishonesty we had to worry abut from the President was about his personal life and not national security, the economy or health care?) To return to the central point, I hope you will still think that you need me and be willing to—metaphorically—feed me…So in almost the exact words of Sir Paul McCartney:

> *Give me your answer,*
> *Fill in a form,*

Mine forever more
Will you still need me,
Will you still feed me,
Now I'm sixty-four?"

—2004

◆　　　◆　　　◆

"I have never really believed that it is more blessed to give than to receive, and I think that is far too easy a way for politicians like myself, who are frequently asking others for money, to assuage our guilt. But I do believe that it is harder to acknowledge receipt than to offer a gift. In fact, it has always seemed to me that when you are giving someone something of value, especially money, nothing more eloquent than 'here' is required. But expressing appreciation as a recipient is a lot harder, especially when you've been doing it for more than thirty years, and I've used up pretty much all of the words suitable to the task...So while my 'thank you' may not soar in terms of prose style, I hope you understand how extraordinarily important this opportunity is for me and how concomitantly grateful I am for your part in it."

—2004

Frankly the best

Barney Frank is both the brainiest and fu
member of Congress, according to the Ju
sue of Washingtonian magazine. The D.C
monthly surveyed senior congressional s
ers' opinions of the best and worst amor
country's top elect-
in b-

Frank gets in t

DURING THE EMOTIO
sometimes raucous c
abortion amendment, m
the Massachusetts deleg
missing. They didn't ta
debate. They didn't eve
chambers. They just q
-

Barney Frank urge
casino pact appro

BOSTON —Decrying
preaching" and "cultura
against gambling, southe
Massachusetts officials urged the
Legislature to ignore opposition
to the W
propose
"A lot
gamblir
Rep. Ba
tive cor
ering tl
with th
"It's n
low-cl
can't

Frank stocking up
as GOP takes aim

THE TEAM RUNNING THE REPUB-
lican Congressional Campaign Committee has made no secret of its yearning to top-
ple one of the most nettlesome House Democrats, Rep. Barney Frank of Newton, in
1996. Never mind that no Republican

By JIM ABRAMS
Associated Press
WASHINGTON — It's been 40
years since House Democrats have
been reduced to backbench s
at a Republican majorit
they've quickly found
crack-
ints of

Wednesday?
"I just want to know what day
this is. I was told we have to do
this on the first day," he said,
referring to the Republican prom-
to pass a host of reforms on the

Frank finds two
bills laughable

A   PROPOSED AMENDMENT TO
the Treasury-Postal Service appropri-
ations bill this week would prohibit membe
of Congress fr   a cost-of-living
raise. Anothe   ored to
kill an execu

Marijuana car
gets Frank boo

WASHINGTON — Con,
uld eliminate federal re
states that allow me
ledical n.

One-of-a-kind politi

The thing about Barney Fr
that he will not be replacec
goes. Frank is one of a kind
smarter than anybody, a
works harder too. He makes
own mind, he's scrupulous
telling the truth, and he d
pocket money that doesn't l
to him. On top of all that, h
been willing to stick with the

Armey, Frank joust
over 'fag' commen

WASHINGTON — Four
infamous slip of the
ity Leader Dich
ney Frank
ns. Arn
restori
ed to the
Barney
t. blan

Frank takes on role
of 'good humor' man

Frank skewers Starr
about investigation

Frank urges
study of drug
legalization

AT. REPRE
WASHINGTON — Rep. Barn
Frank, D-Newton, in a surpr
attack on MX missile funding
st scored a direct hit yester
ils effort to scrap 12 mis-
$1.7 billion.
ass, Frank succeede
silling message
: Presiden
m-Rud-
icks

Frank surprise MX attack
nearly scraps 12 missiles

This
The idea that the all-Democratic Massachusetts
delegation would hire Boston media consultant Michael Gol
man to help them and the
attacks by Cellucci
US Ra

Frank puts leash on attack-dog pla

state party defend themselves fron
ly dead.

Frank, expressing "surprise" be
versations, said he opposes the
"o" impact and there is no need
wer. "ui   that he had not
an item in
un.

CAMBRIDGE (AP) — Rep. Barney Frank
said the U.S. government spends too much
money on jailing people for drug possessic
and small-scale drug dealing, crimes he calle
victim-less.
    Instead, Frank, D-Mass, said the Unite
States should put its limited resources towar
drug treatment programs, which are "under
funded, overstressed and overcrowded."
    "We haven't given those treatment pro
grams a fair chance," he said.
    Frank, who advocates studies on legalizing
drugs, was one of the speakers at a Harvarc
Law School conference titled, "Crime, Drugs,
Health and Prohibition." About 250 people attended the day-long conference Saturday to
talk about anti-drug laws and whether they
should exist.
    He also said the government spends too
much money on stopping drug trafficking at
U.S. borders.
    Sponsors of the conference included the
law school's Criminal Justice Institute, the
Civil Liberties Union of Massachusetts

Frank won't accept award
from rental housing unit

US Rep. Barney Frank (D-Mass.) yesterday
abruptly decided not to accept an award he
was scheduled to receive along with Boston real
estate investor and developer
from the Greater Bost
Rental Housing Assoc.
    Frank had been sel
sociation's Excellence
and Rappaport, the I'
during an annual dinne
ter Dec.1.
    Frank said yesterd
Rappaport was include
cisely because my work l
Association is based on n.   ght or providing
more and better housing for people of low an

Frank hits Helms
on AIDS position

WASHING
Frank, a
called on GOF
yesterday to c
Jesse Helms t
for AIDS res

Capitol spoof gets
Frank portrayal

DURING HIS SUMMER VACATI
last month, Representative Barne
Frank, a Newton Democrat, flew to I
vood to make a cameo appearance o
tion-comedy starri
in J

3

Gay Rights & Related Issues

Barney Frank was the first openly gay member of Congress. This ground-breaking revelation began an unanticipated future for him as a national spokesperson for issues such as gay rights, AIDS funding, gay marriage and civil unions. National elections are now using the gay marriage issue in proposing a constitutional amendment affecting change in a possible ban for gay couples in marriage. These issues have emerged into a major national debate and Congressman Frank has taken a leadership role in advocating gay rights issues.

It should also be noted that Frank was involved in 1989 with a male prostitute and was a victim of bad publicity because of this involvement. Frank, to his credit, demanded an investigation by the House Ethics Committee which largely cleared him of serious charges. He was reprimanded for admittedly taking care of parking tickets for this individual. His political career was salvaged by his open admissions and the fact that he took corrective action in evicting the prostitute when he originally learned of his actions by his landlady. Subsequently, there was no coverup and no crime was committed. Today, Barney Frank's career and reputation has been enhanced as he has taken a leadership role on several congressional committees and was chosen as a point man for the Democrats in the impeachment process of President Bill Clinton.

Barney Frank first broke the news about being a homosexual when a *Boston Globe* reporter asked him his orientation.

"Yes, so what?...I don't think my sex life is relevant to my job."

—1987

◆   ◆   ◆

When Frank learned that Stephen Gobie was using his apartment to run a call-boy, call-girl ring from his apartment, Frank was outraged.

"Thinking I was going to be Henry Higgins and trying to turn him into Pygmalion was the biggest mistake I've made."

—1989

◆   ◆   ◆

When Congressman Frank received word that the *Boston Globe* editorial would call for his resignation, he released a statement rejecting the suggestion.

"I made clear when I requested the ethics committee investigation, and in all my subsequent statements, that I would cooperate fully to ensure that the public knows the facts. I will not take any action which evades that proceeding, and that includes resignation."

—1989

◆   ◆   ◆

"Last time I checked, being stupid wasn't a violation of the rules."

—1999

◆   ◆   ◆

When asked by *Newsweek* magazine if he was threatened by Gobie by blackmail, Frank was forthright.

> *"I know people think closeted gay people can be blackmailed...(But) there are no cases where people betrayed the country because of homosexuality..."*

—1989

◆   ◆   ◆

In defending President Clinton, Frank was asked if he was worried about defending his own personal public life.

> *"I was post-scandal. It would have been hard to blackmail me because all of the embarrassing stuff on me was out. If I were still closeted, that would have been a problem."*

—2001

◆   ◆   ◆

In further comments in an interview with *Newsweek* magazine Frank gave his personal feelings and comments.

> *"In my personal life, I was easy to con. I don't think anybody thinks I'm easy to con in my public life. I said to myself a long time ago: This is a great job if I can do what I think is right. If I can't, I'll bag it. I don't take my district for granted."*

—1989

◆   ◆   ◆

"This is not a moment of self-congratulation for me. Having been accused of a couple of dumb things, one careless one and four outrageous ones, I got it down to one dumb one and one careless."

—1990

◆   ◆   ◆

"A public life cannot substitute for the absence of a private life and in fact if a public life is made to carry too much of an emotional freight it can be distorting."

—1989

◆   ◆   ◆

When Frank's nemesis, Speaker Newt Gingrich, was facing his own ethics charges, Frank was asked his opinion about the upcoming hearings.

"My own personal feelings are too strong to trust my judgment. I will support what the ethics committee does."

—1997

◆   ◆   ◆

In the same interview, Frank explained his stance on naming other homosexual legislators if hypocrisy became an issue on the defense of gay rights.

"I threatened to name the names of gay-bashers…They're entitled to privacy, but they're not entitled to hypocrisy. You can't vote for the 55-mile-per-hour speed limit vote and drive 80 mph. If Jimmy Swaggart wants to go to a motel room with some other woman, I'm not going to pay much attention to it—unless it's Jimmy Swaggart who

has made millions of dollars anathematizing other people from even thinking about doing the same thing."

—1989

◆　　◆　　◆

In other interviews during this period, Frank expounds his views on homosexual topics.

"They're (congressional opponents) saying that my ability to marry another man somehow jeopardizes heterosexual marriage. Then they go out and cheat on their wives. That doesn't jeopardize heterosexual marriage? It's nonsense."

—1999

◆　　◆　　◆

"I don't think my sex life is relevant to my job, but...I don't want to leave the impression that I'm embarrassed by it."

—1999

◆　　◆　　◆

"...I did decide I didn't want to run again...Finally I agreed to poll my district to determine whether or not I should run. The results were that I should. People thought I had behaved stupidly, but they wanted me to run."

—1999

◆   ◆   ◆

"Gay people have a different role than other minority groups... Very few black kids have ever had to worry about telling their parents that they were black."

—1995

◆   ◆   ◆

"I don't know anyone who chose their sexual orientation."

—2004

◆   ◆   ◆

"If Congress had passed a law declaring that if you're gay you're a security risk, I would submit the names of all the gay Republicans I know who would then officially be a security risk...being a gay politician does (not) mean giving up certain freedoms that other people take for granted."

—1999

◆   ◆   ◆

"I find it easier today to defend being gay than to defend being a liberal Democrat."

—2001

◆   ◆   ◆

When asked if he's worried that in light of the Clinton impeachment revelations and his own background what would be the fallout, Frank responded:

"People say, 'Aren't you afraid everyone's sex life will be made public?' I say, 'Hey, I gave at the office.'"

—1999

◆   ◆   ◆

"(U)ntil the early eighties the only votes taken in Congress on matters of sexual orientation involved successful efforts by demagogues and bigots to restrict homosexuals from participating in some government programs."

—1992

◆   ◆   ◆

"No organization has had more impact in its lobbying and educational work against anti-homosexual policies than Parents and Friends of Lesbians and Gays. Few politicians want to argue with a father asserting his right to love his daughter as much as anyone else in America."

—1992

◆   ◆   ◆

After the Presidential election of 2004 where cultural values and the divisive issue of gay marriage was a major factor, Frank spoke to this issue at a public forum.

"There's something to be said for cultural respect. Showing a bit of respect for cultural values with which you disagree is not a bad thing. Don't call people bigots and fools just because you disagree with them."

—2004

◆   ◆   ◆

President George W. Bush gave a press conference announcing he would seek a Constitutional Amendment to make gay marriage unconstitutional and confirm that legal marriage be only defined by a man and a woman. Frank was quick to respond.

"Faced with bad news on virtually every important policy front—Iraq, North Korea, Liberia, the deficit, unemployment, congressional deadlock on prescription drugs—President Bush has taken the advice of his chief advisor, Mr. Rove, and tried to change the subject...Americans should be seriously worried about the prospect that two men who love each other might be allowed to become legally and financially responsible for each other."

—2003

◆   ◆   ◆

When a New York district attorney decided to indict the mayor of New Paltz for his role in gay marriages, Frank strongly objected to this tactic.

"...I fully respect the right of those who object to same-sex marriage to make their case in the courts...But this is not remotely a justification for using the criminal process as a weapon in what is a legitimate political and philosophical debate...because I do not believe that the New York criminal justice system is prepared to convince individuals of the new crime of 'conspiracy to commit commitment...'"

—2004

◆   ◆   ◆

"When did love become a threat?"

—2004

◆   ◆   ◆

"During my years in elected office, I have been involved in a number of debates involving measures that deal with discrimination...In every case, opponents of the legislation have made predictions that social chaos will ensue. In no case of which I am aware have these predictions turned out to be accurate...vivid forecasts of social upheaval, moral decay, interference with the legitimate rights of the majority of people to go about their business, the destruction of important social institutions, and other negative effects; then, after adoption of the cause of all this worry, none of the above."

—2004

◆   ◆   ◆

"I first started filing gay right bills in the Massachusetts legislature in 1972, when I was first elected to the legislature. And at that point, the bigots were honest. They would say, 'We don't want to hire fags. We don't want some dyke working for us. We want to be able to fire them.' Now, they say, 'Oh, well, of course you wouldn't fire someone for being a lesbian, but they're just trying to get special rights.' That is nonsense. There is nothing about anti-discrimination legislation that is 'special' rights—unless you think that's true for blacks, or for Catholics, or Jews or whatever."

—2003

◆   ◆   ◆

When Barney Frank openly stated to the media he was gay, a Massachusetts Republican was the first to make an issue of Frank's orientation. Frank brushed this off.

"There are more important issues to people than the sex life of a middle-aged politician. My impression is my constituents are more concerned about whether Reagan gets us into a war in the gulf, stopping aid to the contras, reducing the budget deficit in a responsible fashion and providing catastrophic health insurance to the elderly. It's not easy to be the Republican chairman and represent Ronald Reagan in Bristol County. It's a hard sell. It's easier to talk about my private life."

—1987

◆   ◆   ◆

When Frank was discussing in an interview the merits of double standards on special legislation for hate crimes, he pointed out the double standard of laws against committing a crime against a congressman and an average citizen. It's the difference between a federal offense and a misdemeanor for the same kind of crime, he explained.

"What—the country is going to go into a recession because someone threw a rock at me?"

—2003

◆   ◆   ◆

Frank was asked if he's able to work in Congress with those who've expressed homophobic sentiments.

"...you certainly have to accept disagreements...we have a rule around here that you're not supposed to take things personally, but I take personal things personally...I do not say, 'Oh well, that's just politics' when people make personally bigoted remarks."

—2003

◆   ◆   ◆

A writer for the *New York Times Magazine* wrote that members of the Christian right who were celebrating evangelist, Pat Robertson's 70th birthday were civil; fairly nice; had a sense of humor and didn't seem to be bad people. Frank had an interesting response.

"That's always true...You know, there were all kinds of charming Southerners who beat their slaves. Didn't he see Gone With the Wind?...Remember this is the nut case (Robertson) who said that Orlando was going to have tornadoes, and the terrible plagues of Egypt were going to fall on it [because of hosting gay men and lesbians at Disney World]."

◆   ◆   ◆

When the issue of a federal constitutional amendment to ban gay marriage was introduced by the Bush Administration, it created a storm of controversy and became a presidential debating issue. Barney Frank took on a strong role in speaking out against this proposal.

"It's one thing to be against gay marriage. It's another to say you're going to go far away from your house and stop it someplace else. That becomes something of an antigay activity... We're going to make sure that's the issue they [the Republicans] are going to have to face."

—2003

◆   ◆   ◆

"If the question is, 'Should one state be able to force every other state to do this, should Missouri vote for a constitutional amendment

stopping Massachusetts from doing it?'—I don't know how they answer that one. I think it is as much a difficult issue for them as it is for us."

—2003

"The notion that gay marriage threatens straight marriage is utterly nonsensical."

—1999

When a filmmaker was completing a documentary on Barney Frank's political career, Frank was asked if this would further make him a target for Republicans.

"How would this manifest itself? More right-wing nuts would think ill of me?"

—2001

"The statement that 'homosexuality is incompatible with military service' is incompatible with the truth."

—1993

"People know the difference between their congressmen and Dr. Ruth. They look to me for constituency services, for advocacy...I didn't think I was elected as a sexual role model."

—1987

♦   ♦   ♦

When the Defense of Marriage Act was introduced in Congress, proponents argued that it was needed to protect the institution of marriage. Frank thought this argument was outrageous.

"That argument ought to be made by someone in an institution because it has no logical basis whatsoever. This is a desperate search for a political issue against people who are unpopular. People say this is not political.. No one in the world believes this is not political."

—1996

♦   ♦   ♦

"Within the Republican Party it is still a liability to be too pro-gay…No senator running in 1996 who voted for the gay and lesbian rights bill suffered any electoral damage because of this."

—2003

♦   ♦   ♦

After his first congressional term ended, Massachusetts legislators redistricted Frank's congressional district uniting him to face off with a popular Republican, Margaret Heckler. Frank stunned the pundits by winning a second term. When he was faced with another redistricting plan in 1991, he was asked in an interview how this would affect him.

"I don't see how my reputation can be trashed any further, but I would hate to see myself regarded as residentially promiscuous."

—1991

◆   ◆   ◆

In a televised *Meet the Press* interview, Frank was asked his view on the Defense of Marriage Act proposal.

"Defense of marriage? It's like the old V-8 commercial as though if this act didn't pass, heterosexual men all over the country would say, [smacking his head]— 'I could have married a guy!'"

—1996

◆   ◆   ◆

Opponents of gay marriage have used the argument that approving the legalization of gay marriage would 'promote homosexuality.' Frank has consistently questioned this notion.

"If you gave me a lot of money and told me you want me to promote homosexuality, I don't know what I would do…How would you promote homosexuality? Have, like, a jingle?"

—2001

◆   ◆   ◆

"I wouldn't know how to promote homosexuality. Do I hire Don King?"

—2001

◆   ◆   ◆

"There are right-wingers who denounce what they call the 'gay agenda.' and they are correct because there is an agenda. The agenda is a set of goals to make people free to pursue their own nature without suffering the legal discriminations. Nobody that I know is going

to set laws that people shouldn't dislike gay people. People are free to
dislike gay people or not."

—2001

◆   ◆   ◆

When *Newsweek* magazine interviewed Congressman Frank suggesting that President George W. Bush allowed a gay foreign service officer to become ambassador despite that he was pushing for a constitutional amendment to prevent gay marriage, Frank had this to say:

"He has literally done not one other good thing for gay people. Say-
ing that Bush has been supportive except for gay marriage is a little
bit like saying he's a very nice man except for the time he murdered
somebody. This constitutional amendment is a pretty grievous
assault."

—2004

◆   ◆   ◆

Barney Frank's quip on the full-page ads in national papers featuring 'ex-gays' who claim to have turned straight with Jesus' help (from the *San Francisco Examiner*, 7/17/98):

"Being Jewish, would I have to go through a 24 step program instead
of a 12 step program?"

—1998

◆   ◆   ◆

"I think the opponents of gay marriage really fall into two categories.
A small group of people just don't like gay people. If you don't like
one, you don't like two. It's geometric. The larger percentage are peo-
ple who are generally supportive of equal rights, as they have been in

Massachusetts, but hear these predictions that it's going to be socially very chaotic, and they figure, why take the chance?"

—2004

◆   ◆   ◆

"We've had now, five months of same-sex marriage [in Massachusetts], and I do not think any heterosexual has noticed—unless they live next door to two lesbians and they had to buy them a present."

—2004

DOROTHY AHLE ILLUSTRATION

4

Legislative Issues

In his testimony in Congress for the record, Frank had lots to say about the tactics of the opposition on the Bankruptcy Abuse Prevention and Consumer Protection Act of 2002.

> *"The bill died because some of the Members there were torn between the people opposed to abortion and the people with money. And you would have thought they could have waited until maybe February or March to get back in the graces of the people with money. But apparently the separation anxiety on the Republican side of not being continuously in the bosom, if not the pocket, of large financial interests, was so great that they had to come up with, and let me use the tech-*

nical parliamentary term, the cockamamiest scheme I have ever seen on the floor of a legitimate democratic legislature."

—2002

"But here is the problem. When the bill had a chance to pass, you voted to kill it. Now, when it is dead, you vote to pass it. And I got to say this, I have to ask you this question, I have to ask you this question because I am interested in your techniques. For this you are going to get credit? I mean, if you can persuade, and let me say in tribute, if you can persuade these sophisticated financial people to give you credit for something this phony, then you are selling too cheap. Why do you not get a platinum credit card with negative interest rates?"

—2002

"Mr. Speaker, as I realized how much time was going to be wasted on this effort to allow some Members to get back in the graces of some of their financial supporters whom they had to alienate, and as we were lionizing, justifiably, Mr. Morris, the refrain kept going through my head. Hey, Mr. Tally Clerk, tally up our votes; daylight comes and we want to go home."

—2002

Barney Frank will occasionally acknowledge and compliment his political adversaries when he feels they've acted fair on their motives or actions.

"Mr. Speaker, I congratulate the members of this committee for the product and the way in which they have done it. I was particularly impressed by the very gracious remarks of the chairman of this committee about his opposite, the ranking minority member, and frankly at a time when there is some political sniping going on that seems to me wholly inaccurate, having him so generously acknowledge the important role the gentlewoman from California (Ms. Pelosi) has played...I should underline that what we have here is the gentlewoman from California in her role on this committee having played a wholly responsible constructive role at the center of national policy. I would ask people to contrast that with some of the silly political assassination efforts that are going on."

—2002

◆　　◆　　◆

Frank made the case for religious discrimination when President George W. Bush made the announcement that he would allow HUD taxpayer funds to religious institutions for secular purposes.

"Under the president's order, churches, synagogues and mosques will receive federal money to build or rehabilitate housing, shelter the homeless, and provide other important public services with the proviso that they may exclude people who do not share their own religious views from employment with these funds...Why does the president believe that Orthodox Jews should not have to associate with Catholics in building housing? How does it hurt Baptists if they have to hire Episcopalians to help feed people? Why does the president believe that Muslims should be able to refuse employment to Jews or Mormons in running recreational programs? What the president is doing here is attempting to short-circuit the legislative process."

—2003

◆   ◆   ◆

In the aftermath of corporate and Wall St. scandals, President Bush in 2002 publicly supported a new law seeking corporate accountability. When things didn't turn out as expected, Frank lambasted the administration and congress.

> *"In July of this year, President Bush signed the law seeking to improve corporate accountability. Unfortunately, in the ensuing five months, the president and his administration have through a combination of lack of interest, covert opposition, and incompetence, deconstructed the Act...A key part of that law was the Public Company Accounting Oversight Board. Today, the board has a chairman who has announced his resignation, and four members with no staff, no office, no telephones, and no real capacity to do their jobs."*
>
> —2002

◆   ◆   ◆

> *"Taken together with the failed appointments that this administration has made to both the SEC and the Accounting Oversight Board, this opposition to adequate funding for either entity has led us into the present situation in which, apparently to the satisfaction of many in the Republican party and some of their business community allies, the legislative effort for increased corporate accountability remains an unrealized hope."*
>
> —2002

◆   ◆   ◆

One of the controversial bills proposed, which Congressman Frank does not shy away from, was the States' Rights to Medical Marijuana Act, a bill he introduced to permit states to allow the use of marijuana for medicinal purposes.

"This is an issue on which people around the country are ahead of the politicians...this is a common sense idea that will give some people who are suffering a measure of relief."

—2002

◆   ◆   ◆

"If you and twelve friends call your representatives every month and let them know that you feel strongly about this issue, we can change this law."

—2001

◆   ◆   ◆

"If there are doctors willing to recommend the use of marijuana for their patients, and states willing to permit it, I think it's wrong for the federal government to subject either the doctors or the patients to criminal prosecution...I would add that taking legal action against those who use small quantities of marijuana for medical purposes is a highly questionable use of scarce prosecutorial resources at a time when they could be put to much better use."

—2002

◆   ◆   ◆

One of Barney Frank's fortes is pointing out hypocrisy in congress, especially when it suits the opposition party's advantage. With his sharp memory for previous votes on various issues, Frank will point out these conflicting points at hand. Here, Frank is criticizing a bill (Gramm-Leach-Bliley Law) permitting insurance firms to reorganize in other states to avoid payments to policyholders.

"My conservative colleagues hypocritically invoke states rights when it advances their ideology, but this provision overriding state insur-

ance laws seeking to protect policyholders is a blatant violation of state decision-making power, and it should be repealed."

—2002

◆   ◆   ◆

The debate on campaign finance reform was an explosive issue for both parties in congress. In debating this issue, which Frank supported, the issue of free speech and hypocrisy by foes of this legislation was again pointed out.

"I have heard people say, on the Republican side mostly, we cannot go ahead with that kind of a forum; if we get rid of soft money, the next thing we know, labor and environmentalists and all those people will dominate the election. We have, in fact, had people almost explicitly say that the danger in campaign finance reform is that the people will have too much to say…there are Members who have supported virtually every restriction on free speech, including censorship on the Internet and other rules the Supreme Court has thrown out, and they have voted for them cheerfully, but when it comes to the power of money to swamp the equal part of our political system, suddenly they become advocates of free speech. Indeed, it seems that many of them are for free speech as long as it is not free. They are for free speech when it costs money, when they can buy it."

—2002

◆   ◆   ◆

"The key is this: They (the opposition) are for free speech as long as it is not free. If you pay for the speech, they are for it. Free free speech they never defend, but paid free speech is something that many of these people find acceptable."

—2002

◆　　　◆　　　◆

In continuing the argument about campaign reform legislation, an amendment was proposed to put this bill's (Shays-Meehan) amendment, which now allows for soft money, into immediate effect before the national election. Frank pointed out the hypocrisy.

> *"Members can differ about a lot of this bill, but it is simply not logically possible to argue that they are for this bill and are going to have it go into effect 3 weeks before primaries which have been conducted heretofore under the old rule. That is just not arguable, and to have someone say I am for the bill but I want to make it take effect right away and then call me a hypocrite is like being called silly by the Three Stooges."*

—2002

◆　　　◆　　　◆

Another area of hypocrisy which Frank had pointed out was the justification of a Bush administration tax cut because the economy was so strong that it was producing more revenue than was needed. A year later, the rationale changed for a tax cut because it was the weakness of the economy that a tax cut was needed to stimulate the economy to avoid a recession.

> *"One of the impressive feats of intellectual tenacity in recent times is the Republicans' ability to sustain their faith in large tax cuts for the wealthy despite repeated battering from reality…In short, the notion that government needs significant shrinkage (which was the only consistent rationale for the Bush tax cut) no longer commands the support it once did—even from the Bush administration. And I doubt that even the most passionate government hater on The Wall Street Journal editorial board says to himself on boarding an air-*

plane that he feels much safer knowing that he has a tax cut in his pocket."

—2001

◆   ◆   ◆

The financial collapses of companies like Enron and WorldCom caused investors to lose millions of dollars and shook investors' confidence in U.S. equity markets. When a provision emerged out of a congressional subcommittee which would sharply curtail the states' ability to take strong enforcement actions against Wall Street firms that defraud investors, Frank took great exception.

"This maneuver is further evidence of the hypocrisy in Republicans' claim of their commitment to states' rights. This Administration hasn't protected investors or punished wrongdoers and now the Republican Congress, which last year was dragged kicking and screaming to pass a strong investor protection law, wants to stop the states from aggressively punishing corporate wrongdoing. If they have their way, there won't be anything left to give back to investors."

—2003

◆   ◆   ◆

Spending priorities on programs usually differs largely from both the Democratic and Republican parties. Here, Frank laments on this difference.

"Mr. Speaker, I am always glad to be present at the annual exhibit of inconsistency on the Republican side. When we talk about this bill, first of all, they denounce us for claiming that additional funding is important in showing we support programs. They then go on to brag about how much additional funding they have provided for the programs. I must say I sometimes do agree that simply throwing money at problems is not necessarily a good idea. I just wish I was

not one of the only few Members who thought that yesterday when we did $400 billion in about 3 minutes for the Defense Department, not all of which is exquisitely well spent."

—2003

◆   ◆   ◆

"They talked about the Federal budget as if it had descended from the sky, the House budget resolution; and somehow these wonderful people in the House who would really love to help not build up the backlog on disability found themselves constrained by this thing called the budget. Apparently it came in a horror movie, stepped off the screen and it constrained them. They voted for it. They imposed this restriction on themselves, and that is the game we are playing."

—2003

◆   ◆   ◆

"There is one glaring exception to the Bush administration's eschewing all things French—King Henry IV is their role model. When told that he could not accede to the throne as a Protestant, he converted to Catholicism explaining, 'Paris is worth a mass.' The highest economic policy positions in the Bush administration—after Karl Rove [Bush's political advisor]—are filled by men who once thought poorly of deficits, but enthusiastically accepted positions which require them to defend not only deficits, but policies which prolong and deepen them. Their version of Henry IV is 'Washington is worth a deficit.'"

—2003

◆   ◆   ◆

Frank has constantly warned about the administration's and its supporters' passing of tax breaks during a wartime economy and its long-term effects.

"This artificial chronological separation between the years of not so bad deficits and the years of insupportable deficits is both intellectually flawed and politically revealing...Politically, this argument demonstrates that what is behind the administration's deficit embrace is an ideological and not an economic motivation. What we are seeing here is a political bait and switch operation...The movie that the conservatives are now producing—'How I Learned To Stop Worrying And Love The Deficit'—ends like its predecessor with a huge explosion, but in this script, it is the notion that the pubic sector has an important role to play in approving the quality of our lives that gets blown up."

—2003

◆   ◆   ◆

Protecting Social Security, Frank argues, is in jeopardy because of the approved tax cuts despite the ongoing deficits.

"The basic logical structure of this argument is that of the joke in which a man falls from the top of a fifty-story building and when asked how he is doing, replies 'Fine so far.' Deficits cumulate...The 'fine so far' argument is that there will be no negative effect as we accumulate trillions of dollars of deficits between now and 2013, but that debilitating impacts on the economy will suddenly appear in 2014 when people read the latest Social Security actuarial tables."

—2003

◆   ◆   ◆

In a public debate on whether the government should fund the Arts, Frank explained why supporting the Arts ought to be a proper role of the government.

"The government picks and chooses which scientific research it backs, and that is not an issue. Funding the Arts is entirely consistent with the principles of democracy...Killing funding would not destroy art but it would hurt people at the margins. Government does have a role in deciding what is a good activity and what is a bad activity, and that is an inescapable role."

—1995

◆   ◆   ◆

In most election years, the issue of flag desecration becomes a wedge issue between parties where the Republican party wants to make a constitutional amendment to make it a crime to "desecrate" the American flag. Frank is opposed to the amendment and constantly makes his argument against the amendment..

"Under this amendment, what will be desecration and punishable in one state may not be in another. Would it be a violation of law to write on the flag, 'I do not respect the government that employs jack-booted thugs to oppress the people?'"—Thus quoting the language of the National Rifle Association, (a favorite Republican lobby) used in a direct-mail appeal.

—1995

◆   ◆   ◆

In showing that the arguments for desecration was a travesty, Frank piled argument upon argument.

"What if you morph the American flag into something that is despicable?"

—1995

◆   ◆   ◆

When a scientist advised Frank that opponents in congress would support the Star Wars defense initiative because it would protect the United States from nuclear terrorism, Frank shot back.

"Why should they do that? We don't have interstellar Shiites."

—1985

◆   ◆   ◆

During a debate on special tax breaks for oil producers, a Texas congressman warned Frank that 'the eyes of Texas are upon you.'

"I don't mind the eyes of Texas being on me, I object to the hands of Texas being in my pockets."

—1985

◆   ◆   ◆

One of Frank's constant statements is in the portraying of partisan differences in bills and philosophy. Here, Frank makes it clear of this difference.

"The gentleman who spoke said this is a Republican Party and he is proud of it. I think there is too good of appreciation in the country today of the real differences that exist between the parties. Partisanship is not always a bad thing. There is a legitimate aspect in a democratic society to recognizing differences. The gentleman from Texas is proud that they passed a tax bill that excluded the poorest working

people in America. He said he is proud of it, and I think we are proud on our side to be appalled by it."

—2003

◆　　　◆　　　◆

"Mr. Speaker, I congratulate the gentleman from Texas in the discretion he showed in continuing to avoid defending this outrageous decision to stiff the poor people."

—2003

◆　　　◆　　　◆

Frank continues to oppose the policy of tax cuts for those with higher incomes.

"When it comes to inequality in the society, there is, of course, the story about a man who goes to the doctor and says, Doctor, when I hold my arm this way it hurts, and the doctor looks and looks and cannot find anything wrong, and he says, okay. I know what to do. He says what? Do not hold your arm that way. I mean, to a certain extent, you can remedy something by simply not continuing to do it. We can stop changing the Tax Code in ways that exacerbate inequality…I would just say in closing to my conservative friends, who are currently and I hope temporarily in control, you have the ability to say no to all these things."

—2004

◆　　　◆　　　◆

Frank has been against the idea of term limits and spoke out against the Term Limit Bill and its hypocrisy.

"Never have so many voted Yes but prayed for a No vote."

—1995

◆   ◆   ◆

Speaking at a graduation ceremony, Frank spoke on the limits of the free market system and refuted the economic metaphor, 'a rising tide lifts all boats.'

"Not everyone has a boat, and if you are standing tiptoe in the water, a rising tide is not good news."

—1987

◆   ◆   ◆

When the Massachusetts legislature was debating the possibility of depressing the Central Artery and its problems and costs, Frank put it in perspective.

"It would be cheaper to raise the city."

—1987

◆   ◆   ◆

After a long session with a new Republican-majority congress, which went well after midnight, Frank spoke up to the day's activities.

"You told us you would be family-friendly. You forgot to tell us it would be the Addams family!"

—1995

◆   ◆   ◆

Frank commented on the controversy about a bill in the House allowing airline pilots and copilots being armed in the cockpit.

"These are people I trust with the lives of 300 human beings. Why am I worried that one might have a pistol?"

—2002

◆   ◆   ◆

During the Whitewater hearings the Chairman of the House Banking Committee pleaded with colleagues to not demean or ridicule one another. Frank rose to object.

"I will give up demean, but do we really have to give up ridicule?"

—1994

◆   ◆   ◆

Frank criticized President Bush for the funding of weapons he felt were unneeded. Frank singled out the F-22 stealth fighter.

"Who are we hiding it from, the Taliban? When people put bombs in their shoes, we don't need to spend money on missile defense."

—2002

◆   ◆   ◆

Frank has often criticized moderate Republicans in congress for giving in to the militant right wing of their party on certain party-line votes.

"It's the moderate Republican three-step: Ineffectual protest, followed by abject surrender, followed by denial."

—1998

In the early 1990s, there was a check-bouncing scandal involving certain members of congress. During a radio interview, Frank was asked about his own checking account policy.

> *"I'm sure my accounts weren't always in order…I chose to keep my accounts in Massachusetts and paid the same fees as a private citizen. Therefore, I chose to do my check—bouncing in my home state to stimulate the economy there."*

—1992

The Gingrich-led GOP targeted Frank for defeat since he was one of the most vocal opponents against the Contract With America legislation, voting for only five of its twenty agenda items.

> *"I've been in my district a lot since the contract was revealed, and if they want an election against me to be a referendum on the contract, I think that's fine. I have spent much more time defending myself for the times I voted with them than for the times I voted against them."*

—1995

When asked if the impeachment hearings on President Clinton was a bipartisan effort, Frank was adamant in his response.

> *"I just want to say that the assertion that this was bipartisan is just silly. If this is bipartisanship, then the Taliban wins a medal for religious tolerance."*

—1998

◆   ◆   ◆

Since a new requirement was put into effect for televised ads by candidates to verbally approve their ads, Frank, in his own words, complied.

> **"I'm Barney Frank, and I approved this message. I mean, who else would?"**

—2004

◆   ◆   ◆

In a battle between developers, politicians and environmentalists, a swamp land in Frank's district was being considered for the building of a shopping mall. Frank saw some humor in the habitat argument since the land has been used as a dumping ground.

> **"I've seen more wildlife in some apartments I lived in."**

—1986

◆   ◆   ◆

Frank has been a consistent advocate for curbing US arms overseas. After France expressed reluctance to help pay the cost of an expanding NATO, Frank saw this coming.

> **"I'm trying to find out how to say 'I told you so' in French."**

—1997

◆   ◆   ◆

When Barney Frank discovered that his name surfaced in classified FBI files from a letter he wrote in 1989 concerning immigration legislation, he was outraged at the policies being conducted on the type of monitoring by the agency.

"They caught me legislating. Paying secret informants to advise us of public information seems a genuinely stupid idea from a number of perspectives."

—2001

◆   ◆   ◆

When congressional reporters worried about leaks to the media from material from pages of grand jury testimony in closed sessions, Frank felt this was disingenuous, to say the least.

"As the leakees you do not have much credibility. I will predict that you will overcome your misgivings and become willing accomplices to the leakers."

—1998

◆   ◆   ◆

In an interview, Frank was asked about the disparities in the legal system as he viewed it.

"Whenever you have a choice—be rich. Take that as a useful principle."

—1987

◆   ◆   ◆

One of the most common forms of congressional gridlock is also a hallowed tradition by a minority party in congress—the filibuster, which gives the minority party the ability to halt legislation. Barney Frank decided to take on the one tactic which, if passed in congress, would end a Senate debate. When reminded that the filibuster was an American tradition, Frank snapped back:

"Like Slavery."

—1993

◆   ◆   ◆

"…(T)he 1999 debates on Medicare with members expressing their incredulity at the imposed cuts represent the greatest example in history of people expressing shock at the entirely foreseeable consequences of their own actions."

—2000

◆   ◆   ◆

After an appellant court ruling for federal employees with equal employment opportunity complaints was finally processed after a four year wait, Frank made the announcement:

"The good news is: after four years, they've finally processed your complaint. The bad news is: nobody cares."

—1985

◆   ◆   ◆

After a week of House approved resolutions congratulating the Secretary of State, several nations and the display of the Ten Commandments in government offices, Frank quipped about the seriousness of lawmaking.

"We are indeed legislating. We are in a congratulatory legislative mode. This week we will be congratulating Guatemala, Nicaragua, Warren Christopher and Moses."

—1997

◆   ◆   ◆

Unlike other states where publicly financed stadiums have been built for major league franchises, Congressman Frank objected to a proposal by the owner of the New England Patriots football team to build in South Boston.

"The idea that the federal government should be helping wealthy people get wealthier by helping them build a private development is terrible public policy. And people whose average income is $32,000 a year should not be asked to subsidize a stadium, because in the end, that's who would be paying for any such tax break."

—1997

◆   ◆   ◆

When former Attorney General, Richard Thornburgh, decided not to appear at a congressional hearing because he felt the hearings would be confrontational, Frank felt this was basically a political copout.

"This is the House of Representatives, not a church."

—1991

◆   ◆   ◆

When a *Boston Globe* columnist wrote a piece on obesity, Barney Frank couldn't resist updating him on some congressional resolutions.

"You missed the…vote in the House of Representatives denouncing fat. The Republicans asked us to vote for this, to my surprise. This is the kind of broad government mandate they used to be against. It does mention erectile dysfunction, which is sort of unusual for a House resolution."

—2002

◆   ◆   ◆

Frank has consistently been against what he believes are costly and ineffective government subsidy programs. He regarded the subsidies for dairy farmers to reduce production as "guild socialism" and warned that the government would end up "subsidizing everything short of tofu."

> *"[The butter surplus program was so large it could be used] to slather Wyoming into complete slipperiness."*

> —1985

◆   ◆   ◆

Frank responded to President Reagan's proposed major cutbacks, especially to the potential damage to HUD grants on housing.

> *"If those proposals go through, the only federally funded urban program would be Imelda Marcos's property acquisitions in New York."*

> —1986

◆   ◆   ◆

Terrorism tension has always been subject to security measures around Capitol Hill. When Frank forgot his briefcase in the Capitol building and returned to retrieve it, he discovered the area was roped off and the Capitol police were on guard outside the door. Frank was able to retrieve it after he assured police it was his.

> *"Look inside. If it has a pair of sneakers and a week old Washington Post inside you have nothing to fear."*

> —1986

◆   ◆   ◆

Responding to the polls that the American public wants their programs, but is reluctant to pay for them in increased taxes, Frank gives his basic answer.

"Everyone wants to go to heaven, but no one wants to die."

—2002

◆   ◆   ◆

When the House passed a faith-based initiative bill which the Democrats opposed, the GOP decided to scale it back so that the Republican Senate would pass its new form. Frank thought it biased for various reasons.

"I thought they'd be thinking about faith in God, not in the Senate."

—2001

◆   ◆   ◆

Barney Frank has occasionally criticized the complaints of conservatives who decry 'judicial activism' when courts render decisions which overturn certain laws which they disagree with.

"You can frame it right underneath the Bush v. Gore opinion, an 'activist' opinion if ever there was one."

—2004

◆   ◆   ◆

"One more try for all those folks who missed it the first three times: When you accuse courts who render decisions which you don't agree with you end up sounding like a bunch of whining babies. And that is exactly how the Republicans who make these charges of Capitol

Hill sound. There is no such 'problem' with the legal system in our country. That is why there is no serious attempt to address the 'problem.'"

—2004

◆　　　◆　　　◆

Frank was displeased about an anti-drug bill passed by the House.

"This bill is the legislative equivalent of crack. It yields a short-term high but does long-term damage to the system and it's expensive to boot."

—1986

◆　　　◆　　　◆

When House Republicans griped over President Clinton's economic plan, Barney Frank turned his talents to being a lyricist and performed the following tune as a recommended Republican theme song:

"Yes, we have no specifics,
We have no specifics today.
We will attack your plan,
And do everything we can,
To bring gridlock back into play.
But we'll offer no detail.
We want only to derail
Your train, and create disarray.
We will propose no cuts.
That's politically nuts.
We will have nothing concrete to say.
Yes, we have no specifics.
We have no specifics today."

—1993

ELEANOR MILL ILLUSTRATION

5

Frank Nuggets

"Politics are local, but economics are global."

—1999

◆　　◆　　◆

"I'd rather be rude than bored. A gentleman is never unintentionally rude."

—1999

♦   ♦   ♦

"What I try to do is make people think they're ridiculous and not take them seriously. I think there's a certain value in being very nasty, especially if it's publicly nasty."

—1999

♦   ♦   ♦

"Hey, I'm a left-handed gay Jew. I've never felt, automatically, a member of any majority." The New Republic (c)

—1996

♦   ♦   ♦

"Very few members of Congress refuse to meet with their constituents. I mean, being a member of Congress and refusing to meet your constituents is kind of like being a shoe salesman and not wanting to talk to the customers."

—2000

♦   ♦   ♦

"...just tell [your congressman] what you think. And do it in your own letter. Don't sign a petition by the way, that's a horseshit way to do it, write them a letter. Don't fill out a postcard that's preprinted. That has less effect. Because what we're trying to persuade the member of Congress is that this is something you really care about. And the way to do that is for you to write an individual letter. Letters are even better than phone calls."

—2000

◆   ◆   ◆

"One of the impressive feats of intellectual tenacity in recent times is the Republicans' ability to sustain their faith in large tax cuts for the wealthy despite repeated battering from reality."

—2001

◆   ◆   ◆

"Those who oppose abortion while voting against infant-nutrition programs believe life begins at conception and ends at birth."

—1989

◆   ◆   ◆

"[The Democrats] biggest problem over the last twenty years was our identification with crazies on the Left."

—1995

◆   ◆   ◆

"I think a large part of the public likes the conservatives' theme music. Now they will be tested on whether they like the lyrics."

—2004

◆   ◆   ◆

"Anyone who professes respect, devotion and the honoring of Dr. King's memory and doesn't vote is a liar."

—2004

◆　　◆　　◆

"It is our job to refute those who would try to defang Dr. King's biting ideology. Don't just keep alive the memory of Dr. King, but do the work of Dr. King."

—2004

◆　　◆　　◆

"By the way, one of the misarguments that is used to defend stiffing the poorest people in this country when the wealthiest are doing very well is, well, they do not pay taxes. Do people in this Chamber really not notice something called the Social Security payroll tax?"

—2003

◆　　◆　　◆

"As the ranking member, let me say I appreciate we have an open rule here. We do have an inverse relationship here. Well, we have two. One, the poorer a person is, the less fairly they are going to be treated in the tax bill. Secondly, the less important the legislation, the more open-handed the Committee on Rules will be in letting us discuss it."

—2003

◆　　◆　　◆

"Let's be very clear: We're capitalists, as we should be. Inequality is not a bad thing. It's necessary to our system. A market system with its incentives and its allocation mechanisms doesn't work without inequality. On the other hand, I think it is clear that inequality left

entirely unchecked might get out of the bounds where it is reasonable. And too much inequality can have serious negative consequences."

—2004

"(T)he extent to which you were going to retrain some 49 or 53 year old with a high school education was limited in terms of its appeal to them; but even to the extent that you were retraining, let us note that the jobs that I was being told 15 years ago, for which we would retrain people, we would not only now have to retrain them, we would have to buy them airplane tickets because they are going out of the country."

—2004

"(A) number of people have asked me if I will receive a flu shot. On the advice of my doctor I had planned on getting the flu shot, like I do every year. However, after the shortage was announced I cancelled my appointment because I do not believe it is appropriate for members of Congress to receive special consideration."

—2004

"The gentleman from California asked what it would be called, what it would be like if our point of order were to prevail. I will answer him. It would be called democracy. I ask that the majority

not in the name of defending democracy throughout the world extinguish it here on the floor of the House of Representatives."

—2002

◆   ◆   ◆

"The notion that partisanship is bad really ignores the history of democracy. Parties are not a bad thing; they are not something that people put on earth to corrupt the political process. Parties are, in fact, a necessary element in self-government. You cannot find a democracy of any size in the history of the world that did not have political parties, and it's not because anybody decided to create them, they just have been organic growth."

—2002

◆   ◆   ◆

"We have two systems in America. We have an economic system—capitalism—that requires inequality. If people are not unequally rewarded, then the capitalism system doesn't function. So you need inequality in our economic system. We have, side by side, a political system that is based on equality—one person, one vote—now you don't have one person, one dollar; that wouldn't work. But you do have one person, one vote. To the extent that money has come to have more of a role in our political process, the unequal element of the society has overshadowed the equal element. What you really want is a tension between the two; you want the inequality of the capitalist system and the more equalizing element of the political system working together."

—2002

◆   ◆   ◆

"Well, I—this is going to be a boring show, Chris, (<u>Hardball</u> on MSNBC—TV) because once again I agree with you completely."

—2002

◆   ◆   ◆

"(W)hile on the subject of the power of words, I want also to express my disagreement with the decision to construct an awkward title for this bill so that it yields the acronym "PATRIOT." Only my strong commitment to freedom of expression in general keeps me from filing legislation to ban the use of acronyms in general in legislative work...But invoking the PATRIOT in the context of this bill gives the unfortunate impression that those who disagree with it are not patriots."

—2002

◆   ◆   ◆

"(T)he people who are losing their jobs and feeling the pain and losing their health care and having their pensions jeopardized do not, in this case, feel as persuaded by Joseph Schumpeter's argument about creative destruction as they instinctively tend to understand what John Maynard Keynes said when he argued to people who said do not worry about what is happening now, it will be better in the long run. In the long run, we shall all be dead..."

—2004

◆   ◆   ◆

"I recognize dwelling simply on the moral aspects and the social costs of inequality may not be enough. As Adlai Stevenson once said, when he was told he had all the thinking people on his side, 'Yes, but I need a majority.' Of course, it was cracks like that helped him not get a majority. But I don't unfortunately, believe the moral argument is enough…I believe the reality—that the owners of capital are getting a disproportionately unequal share, damagingly so, of the gains."

—2004

◆   ◆   ◆

"(L)et me give you my philosophy. I am a capitalist. I believe the free enterprise system is the best way to create wealth. That means I welcome some inequality in the system. If you do not have inequality, if people are not unequally rewarded for their skills, for their energy, for their correct guesses or intuitions about what the public will want, then the system does not work. But I also believe that left entirely to its own, as I thought we had decided as a country with Franklin Roosevelt, more inequality will be generated than is either socially healthy or economically necessary."

—2004

◆   ◆   ◆

"I had my first heart attack after I was involved in my own set of accusations so maybe there is a correlation between sex-related scandals and heart attacks—in which case I hope everybody will behave. It gives the phrase 'affairs of the heart' a new meaning."

—1999

◆   ◆   ◆

"Votes beat money any day in the American system. If there is a divergence between the sentiment of your contributors and the sentiments of your voters, the voters win every time."

—1997

◆   ◆   ◆

"Our present defense budget makes sense only if you believe Hungary will invade France."

—1990

◆   ◆   ◆

"We're the only people I know who are expected to take large amounts of money from perfect strangers and have it have no effect on our behavior."

—2000

◆   ◆   ◆

"Raising funds politically is—taking a sum of money and then developing amnesia."

—1990

◆　　◆　　◆

"[Racism] is the single continuing flaw in this country. The crazies feed on each other. And those of us looking on think the crazies speak for their sides. They don't."

—1984

◆　　◆　　◆

"People don't want to hear about abortion and other people's sex lives during dinner. Television is an intrusive medium."

—1984

◆　　◆　　◆

"We [politicians] give more straight answers than the general public."

—1984

◆　　◆　　◆

"Voting, as many of my colleagues know, is not heavy lifting."

—1999

◆　　◆　　◆

"Jimmy Carter and Ronald Reagan both sold advanced weapons to Saudi Arabia and Congress went along, despite strong objections from Israel and many of Israel's supporters in the US. America still does not recognize the Israeli capital of Jerusalem—indeed, if Amer-

ican foreign policy personnel do take orders from Jerusalem, they apparently insist that these orders be routed by way of Tel Aviv."

—1985

"We make rules that tie us up in knots, so when we're asked to do something we can say, 'Gee, I'd like to help you out, but I'm all tied up in knots."

—1986

"Judges usurp the power of legislative bodies, but that's because the legislators want it that way."

—1986

"You never have the right to lie, but you don't have to volunteer the truth all the time."

—1986

"It's a mistake for politicians to comment on the press, because they're not going to give honest answers."

—1986

◆   ◆   ◆

"When people say, 'What can I do about this—about that issue', I say 'Throw them out in November', it's as simple as that."

—2004

◆   ◆   ◆

"They [Republicans] don't win by cheating—except in Florida—they win because people sit home on their asses."

—2004

◆   ◆   ◆

"The best organization we have on all the important issues is Organized Labor."

—2004

◆   ◆   ◆

"You are not legally responsible for your relatives—a fact for which my relatives are glad."

—1991

◆   ◆   ◆

"I do think the average member of Congress overwhelmingly is well-motivated. Most members of Congress are really there because they want to do what they think is the right thing for the world, though I

don't agree with some of their views. But there's also less perfection, there's a lot more human emotion and error."

—2003

◆   ◆   ◆

"Free speech means freedom for the obnoxious, jerks and the stupid."

—1995

◆   ◆   ◆

"Today's vote on term limits have many voting yes and praying no. This is an issue with a lot of lip service and no teeth."

—1995

◆   ◆   ◆

"If military spending isn't reduced, then we have zero chance of reducing the budget deficit without losing social conscience."

—1996

◆   ◆   ◆

"The Republicans have, for some time now, portrayed themselves as the party of morality and traditional family values. It turns out that lack of perfect behavior is, in fact, bipartisan, across ideological lines. But it is worse in their case because of the hypocrisy."

—2003

◆　　◆　　◆

"Every politician is entitled to privacy, but no politician is entitled to hypocrisy."

—2004

◆　　◆　　◆

"A war in which the Americans do all the dying and all the shooting and all the spending and all the bleeding is not only morally unfair to the American people, it is unwise."

—1991

◆　　◆　　◆

"The organizations that have the most influence in Congress do not engage in civil disobedience. They move members of Congress by a combination of reasoned argument and political power. Civil disobedience is more usually resorted to by people who have no access to power."

—1994

◆　　◆　　◆

"Once—I voted for a perfect candidate—then the next time I voted, I wasn't so perfect. I voted for myself anyway."

—1992

◆   ◆   ◆

"Do I think we should have better candidates—yeah, but I do not know where to order them."

—1992

◆   ◆   ◆

"Anytime someone denigrates the value of money in solving the problem, you are talking to someone that isn't interested in trying to solve that problem. Because, I have never heard any of my conservative colleagues say to me, 'What do you think, you can defend America by throwing money at the Pentagon?' You don't get to the moon or the stars without spending money."

—1998

◆   ◆   ◆

"(T)here are probably some people who, no matter how much opportunity we give to them, aren't going to do well. There are people who are born with less capability than some of the rest of us, and the penalty of this country for not being able to make your way in your world, for not being bright and articulate and well integrated, shouldn't be starvation and misery…"

—1998

◆   ◆   ◆

"I never robbed a bank, either. I think it's a pretty stupid question. You guys are making it an issue. Whether or not someone smoked marijuana in college is not an issue."

—1990

◆   ◆   ◆

"(T)he First Amendment guarantees people's rights to make anti-gay, anti-Jewish, anti-black and anti-Catholic remarks. Are you saying it's OK to offend Catholics and not Jews? Laws don't protect just minorities, they protect everyone. The notion that the less powerful are protected by the government against attacks by the more powerful, but that it's not reciprocal, is nonsense..."

—1990

◆   ◆   ◆

"We must defend hateful people's right to be hateful."

—1990

◆   ◆   ◆

"Do you now denounce 'activist judges'? What are judges—pirates?"

—2004

◆   ◆   ◆

"The best argument for refusing President Bush's request that we put America $87 billion deeper in debt to pay for the mistakes he has made in Iraq comes from a very good source—George W. Bush."

—2003

◆   ◆   ◆

"We're all candidates all the time. Claude Pepper is eighty-seven, and he's worried about redistricting in 1992."

—1988

◆   ◆   ◆

"I think it's entirely compatible for liberals to be responsible—I'm a liberal."

—1987

◆   ◆   ◆

"I'd rather have a prison next door to me than an elementary school. If the prisoners get out, they leave as fast as they can. If the kids get out, they just want to hang around and get into trouble."

—1986

◆   ◆   ◆

"Some people of limited means make unwise spending choices about such things as cars, cigarettes and alcohol. Many middle and upper income people get into financial trouble because of credit card abuse

or poor investments. Our response in each case should be reasonable regulation and consumer education—not outright restrictions on choices with which we disagree."

—1997

◆　　◆　　◆

"(T)he reason the gambling casino is so enthusiastically supported by a majority of people in the Bristol County area is that it will provide jobs, not that they expect to hit the jackpot."

—1997

◆　　◆　　◆

"(C)onsider the inconsistency here. The appropriate liberal approach is to give people as much education as possible, to make sure they have access to all the institutions that will help them, but not to outlaw some of their choices because we in the more enlightened class think they are unwise."

—1997

◆　　◆　　◆

"[Political drug testing is] a degrading tactic, a cheap trick. I don't think the voters are falling for it. Two politicians urinating in a bottle would have no impact on the drug problem in this society. Those who do it have a total misunderstanding of the drug problem."

—1986

◆   ◆   ◆

"The absence of money means the absence of solutions."

—2002

◆   ◆   ◆

"If you're not able to work closely with people you despise, you can't really work here."

—2000

◆   ◆   ◆

"On virtually every important anti-discrimination issue that has come up, the overwhelming majority of Republicans have voted for discrimination."

—1994

◆   ◆   ◆

"I have not found too many Orthodox Jews who are in favor of prayer in the schools for a very simple reason. Few Jews expect school prayer to be conducted in Hebrew."

—1989

◆   ◆   ◆

"The only difference between a campaign contribution and a bribe is timing."

—1986

◆　　◆　　◆

"The job of the opposition is to call attention to those things that the majority party would just as soon do in the dark."

—1995

◆　　◆　　◆

"The fat of government is not lying on top, but is marbled through the meat."

—1995

◆　　◆　　◆

"Conservatives are terrified by the disappearance of the deficit. They used the deficit as an excuse for being socially irresponsible."

—1999

◆　　◆　　◆

"Democrats usually win when the voters are focusing on issues, and Republicans almost always win when voters are concerned with values."

—1992

◆　　◆　　◆

"A lot of my colleagues think gambling is a little tacky. It's not for me to say, 'That's low-class, that's low rent.' You can't do that."

—1995

◆　　　◆　　　◆

"In reference to 'I don't give a shit—'reporters themselves used this kind of language. Is there a double-standard?"

—1991

◆　　　◆　　　◆

"I understand my reputation for being very liberal, and on a lot of substantive issues, I am. When it comes to freedom of speech, I'd let almost anybody say anything. When it comes to helping poor people, I am very much committed on that. But on crime issues, that has not been the case. I'm not a big civil libertarian on the crime issue."

—1993

◆　　　◆　　　◆

"It's always been a mistake to think that because I have strong ideological commitments, therefore I must be uncompromising."

—1993

◆　　　◆　　　◆

"I don't give a shit about banks. Our job isn't to protect any existing financial institution; it's to protect the economy."

—1991

◆　　　◆　　　◆

"You can't bullshit us on this. If you are not for cutting the military budget, then you are not for these social programs. Reality is on my

side. Every budget from now on will suck. And each one will suck worse, from everybody's perspective except the military's."

—1997

◆　　◆　　◆

"My ambition to get the Ethics Bill passed surpasses my ambition to be quoted about it."

—1988

◆　　◆　　◆

"Taking Eastern Airlines is like the lottery. The odds are better you'll win the lottery than getting to your destination on time."

—1987

◆　　◆　　◆

"I'm starting over again. Basically they gave me a new heart. I've got totally clean arteries. [With shortness of breath] I kept sounding like Marilyn Monroe singing 'Happy Birthday.'"

—1999

◆　　◆　　◆

"Saturday Night Live—I thought the guy who played me was way too fat. I was miffed...but then I saw that the guy who played Maxine Waters was even uglier than the guy who played me, so I realized she had the bigger complaint."

—1998

◆   ◆   ◆

"I still quote [journalist, Murray] Kempton's great line: 'The function of editorial writers is to come down from the hills after the battle is over, and shoot the wounded.' I like to apply that to corporate boards of directors."

—2004

◆   ◆   ◆

"It takes a year to get the legislation through, and it then takes a year for candidates to find the loopholes."

—1994

◆   ◆   ◆

"The best way to win any campaign is before the campaign begins."

—2004

◆   ◆   ◆

"The President has a constitutional right to behave like a spoiled child."

—1989

◆   ◆   ◆

"People have been talking about America's loss of innocence. It's more about our loss of guilt, from Vietnam to colonialism."

—2001

◆   ◆   ◆

"There are three not-sa-pos-tas that have hurt liberals. You're not supposed to say that the free enterprise system is wonderful. You're not supposed to say that, in our era, certainly since the fall of Hitler, communism has been by far the worst system of government in the world or that most people who are in prison are bad people."

—1992

◆   ◆   ◆

"Fallible people should not do irrevocable things if there is any alternative. On the other hand, I never read about a person about to be executed whom I will miss."

—1992

◆   ◆   ◆

After the Gobie scandal broke, *Playboy* magazine asked Frank for a feature interview.

"I said I didn't want to be in <u>Playboy</u>, and they said, 'Oh, but we also want your views on the issues,' I said, 'Why didn't you ask me for my views on the issues last week?"

—1989

◆   ◆   ◆

"When we try to act unilaterally [Republicans] are upset; when we act with our allies, they are upset. When there is no consistency in

the criticism, that's a pretty good indication that it's political [exple-tive]."

—1999

♦   ♦   ♦

"I underspend everything in my allotment except staff. I think people think I'm doing a good job."

—1992

♦   ♦   ♦

"Open meetings and the abolition of proxies are no substitute for will."

—1995

♦   ♦   ♦

"[N]onsense in the service of prejudice is still nonsense, whether spouted by a Senator or a Justice."

—2003

♦   ♦   ♦

"Political movements that insist that good intentions are an accept-able substitute for tough strategic thinking are unlikely to succeed."

—2005

◆   ◆   ◆

"There has been a tremendous amount of resistance [to investigations]. Bureaucracy has a self-protective mechanism. And there's a real reluctance in this country to looking at ourselves in a bad light."

—1985

◆   ◆   ◆

"You know, sitting vice presidents almost always get the nomination when they want to."

—1999

◆   ◆   ◆

"Obviously, people who believe in free speech believe in it no matter what the politics are of those who say it. So when we have this one-sided effort to criticize people who advocate violence or don't preach family values, I am forced to conclude that there is some mysterious ailment in the land which has ended the hearing in the right ear of many of my colleagues."

—1995

◆   ◆   ◆

"The trouble with the Soviets is that they do not attach any independent value to human rights and that makes it difficult for us to make any headway."

—1986

◆   ◆   ◆

"I survive boring meetings by trying not to go to them."

◆   ◆   ◆

"We share this country with 250 million other people. That means you almost never reach a consensus on everything."

—2000

◆   ◆   ◆

"If you're not here to try to make this a better world, you have no business being here."

6

Say, What?

"A rising tide may lift all boats, but if you're in the harbor with no boat, the tide just goes up your nose."

—2002

◆　　◆　　◆

"If you're going to be an effective legislator, the most important principle to remember is that the ankle bone is connected to shoulder bone."

—2003

◆   ◆   ◆

"He left me out! Can you believe this? Oliver North writes up a list of the 25 most dangerous liberals in Washington and he leaves me out!"

—1996

◆   ◆   ◆

"I talk about this with Mr. Greenspan when he testifies. He will cite in his speeches and elsewhere a very eminent deceased economist, Joseph Schumpeter. In his great book, 'Capitalism, Socialism and Democracy,' he talked about creative destruction. He said, you know, he did not say you know. He was an illustrian much more formal than me. Than I. He would not say than me either. Joseph Schumpeter said, when you destroy old economic entities because they are outdated, new ones will be created out of the resources freed up. That is what he means by creative destruction, Mr. Greenspan."

—2004

◆   ◆   ◆

"The gentleman from North Carolina said, why are we objecting? We are giving a tax cut here and a tax break here. There a tax break, here a tax break, everywhere a tax break. I am for many of those; not for all of them. The problem is the attitude that says to the American people, here are some freebies. The one word that people never mention is 'sacrifice.' We are not talking about going around in sackcloth and ashes, whatever those look like. I do not know myself but I have heard that often enough. What we are saying, however, is you cannot have it all...There is a failure here to tell people the truth."

—2002

◆　　　◆　　　◆

"We vote here, but not under oath. Maybe we ought to vote under oath sometimes and not just testify under oath. Everybody is going to vote for this, they tell us, but I do not think it is going to be carried out."

—2002

◆　　　◆　　　◆

"Well, you are responsible when you authorize and write into law for the expenditures that come…So I am glad that people are going to vote with us. I just wish they meant it."

—2002

◆　　　◆　　　◆

"Note the apparent assumption that just because we say something does not mean we mean it. When you say do not worry, this is just an authorization bill calling for the expenditure of these billions, but it does not actually spend them, I am reminded of the couplet from Tom Lehrer that I cannot quite remember, but it did involve Wernher Von Braun, the former German rocket scientist…and I remember the rhyme which was basically he was in this song disclaiming responsibility for the damage his creations had done in England, because, the words went, in effect, I am not responsible. I am only in charge of when they went up. I am not responsible for where they came down, said Wernher Von Braun."

—2002

◆   ◆   ◆

"The jobs now being outsourced are the jobs we used to retrain people for. We just forgot to give them airplane tickets when we gave them retraining."

—2004

◆   ◆   ◆

"If they think it's such a sacrifice to go into public service, then they should stay the heck out."

—1988

◆   ◆   ◆

"I am in the only profession that I know of, where if people have a high degree of consumerism [where incumbency holds a safe seat to be being re-elected]—something is drastically wrong."

—1988

◆   ◆   ◆

"I think that a kinder and gentler approach to accounting than we've had would violate the sodomy laws most states have."

—2002

◆   ◆   ◆

"At the level of pay that those of you who run banks get, why the hell do you need bonuses to do the right thing? Most people in the world don't get bonuses to do the right thing. I mean, do we really have to

bribe you to do your jobs? I'm serious. I don't get it. I don't get a bonus. Cops don't get bonuses...And the problem is not just the bonuses. Think what you're telling the average worker, that you who are the most important people in the system and at the top, that your salary isn't enough, that you need to be given an extra incentive to do your job?"

—2004

◆　　◆　　◆

"With the welfare queen, no one had seen her. And no one knew anyone who had seen her. But a lot of people know someone who knows someone who thinks they've seen her."

—1989

◆　　◆　　◆

"Mr. Speaker, by testing a nuclear weapon later this week, the President is going to take another step toward making any serious arms reduction impossible. In his seventh year, the President has a record of total nonachievement. We have had a lot of 'almosts,' a lot of 'gunna's' a lot of 'nearly's,' and we have had nothing."

—1987

◆　　◆　　◆

"I do not feel I misinterpreted a reasonable instinct. I correctly interpreted an unreasonable instinct."

—1986

◆   ◆   ◆

"The implication that I was unsuccessful in lighting my cigar while lighting my shirt is inaccurate. In fact, I not only succeeded in lighting both but was further able to quickly extinguish the latter while keeping the former burning."

—1998

◆   ◆   ◆

"I said to someone, you don't go far running as a fat, left-handed, Jewish homosexual in America, so the noise you just heard is my closet door slamming shut."

—1989

◆   ◆   ◆

"When they lie about you, you know what to do; it's when they tell the truth about you that it's hard to figure out how to defend yourself."

—1989

"If you wear brown shoes with a blue suit, people think you don't know better. If you wear tennis shoes, they think you're making some sort of statement."

—1986

◆   ◆   ◆

"Someone said to me, 'You're wearing an ill-fitting suit.' I said, 'No, it's not an ill-fitting suit. It's a very well fitting suit. I just don't happen to be the person it fits.'"

—1995

◆   ◆   ◆

"No one ever said that cultural lag isn't a factor with the bureaucracy."

—2001

◆   ◆   ◆

"It's one thing to never do something; it's another to undo it."

—2001

◆   ◆   ◆

"First, unlike the 'lockbox' concept—and the longer I hear that debate carried on, the more I am convinced that if we were to make any change in the First Amendment, it should be to ban the use of metaphors in the discussion of public policy..."

—2001

◆   ◆   ◆

"On the day I die, I'll either be fat or hungry."

—1985

Selected Bibliography

Boston Globe/articles, 1984-2005.
Boston Herald/articles, 1998-1999, 2001-2003.
Washington Post/articles, 1998, 2004.
San Francisco Examiner/article, 1998.
The Daily Item/articles, 1986, 1994, 1999.
The Tab/articles, 1985-1986.
Boston Globe/TGIF, June 25, 1992, Alex Beam
Metro Weekly/Dec. 25, 2003, Year in Review
North Shore Sunday/Feb. 2, 1986, Politics, Howard Iverson
The Boston Phoenix/Oct. 9, 1998, Don't Quote Me, Dan Kennedy
Wellesley Townsman/Oct. 21, 2004
Liberal Opinion Week/Jan. 30, 1995, The 1995 GOP Model of the Pander-Bear, Mark Shields
City Limits magazine/Aug. 1981, Stand-Up Politics, Jay Darby
New York Times magazine/Feb. 4, 1996, And Then There Was Frank, Claudia Dreifus
New York Review of Books/Mar. 23, 1995, The Visionary, Gary Wills
Boston Globe magazine/Dec. 1, 1985, The Fat of the Land, H. Paris Burstyn
    /Brawler on the Hill, May 21, 1995, Bob Hohler
Newsweek/Sept. 25, 1989, Barney Frank's Story, Tom Morganthau, Howard Fineman, Eleanor Clift, Mark Starr, Bill Turque
Mother Jones/May-June 1995, Being Frank, Claudia Dreifus
The New Republic/Mar. 6, 1995, Frank Incensed, Weston Kosova
The American Prospect/Feb. 14, 2000, Taps for Caps, Barney Frank
    /Jan. 29, 2001, Trigger Happy, Barney Frank
    /July 2-16, 2001, Beyond Jeffords, Robert L. Borosage & Roger Hickey
    /Nov. 5, 2001, Repeal Bush's Tax Cut, Barney Frank
    /Feb. 25, 2002, Where's Bill?, Chris Black
The Progressive/Nov. 2000, Barney Frank versus Ralph Nader, Ruth Conniff
    /Mar. 2001, Et Tu, Feingold?, Ruth Conniff

Racine Labor/Aug. 21, 1998, The View from Here, John Nelander
GQ magazine/Sept. 1995, Barney Rubble, John B. Judis
Playboy/July 1999, Interview, David Sheff
Rolling Stone/Feb. 4, 1999, Checking in with Barney Frank, Will Daria
ENDA (End Discrimination Against Gays) Interview/Oct. 28, 1994, Bill Corey
The Advocate/Oct. 14, 1997, A President for Us, Barney Frank
PlanetOut journal/Apr. 28, 2000, An Interview with Barney Frank, Matt Alsdorf
The Voice/June 27, 1989, On Naming Names, Doug Ireland
Gay City News/July 15-21, 2004, article
In These Times/May 29, 1995, Life of the Party, John Canham-Clyne
The Nation/Mar. 24, 1997, A Frank Talk on the Budget, David Corn
Senior Action Leader/Aug. 2002, Wasn't That a Time?, Jack Boesen, editor
Massachusetts Banker/First Quarter, 2003, Frank-ly Speaking, Larry Collins
Massachusetts News/Dec. 1999, Frank Tells Untruths
Newsweek/(MSNBC-Newsweek web exclusive, An Evolution, Christina B. Gillham
George magazine/Feb. 1999, Frankly Barney, Lynn Snowden
Boston Magazine/Dec. 1985, He Looks Mahvelous!, Art Jahnke
          /Feb. 1999, Riders on the Storm, Joe Conason
The Journal (Mass. Jewish weekly)/May 5, 1995, Should Government Fund the Arts?,
Douglas Belkin
The Hoya news journal/Oct. 19, 2001, Frank Discusses U.S. Policy, Attitude Regarding
Gay Rights, Alex Finerman
CWA News/June 1999, Workers' Agenda item, Morton Bahr, editor
CPPAX Newsletter/Aug. 22, 1996, A Peacetime Military Budget, Alysia Ordway
News Releases (B. Frank), 2002-2005
Public Correspondence (B. Frank), 1982-2005
Inside Congressional Politics/Apr. 15, 2002, Interview
Congressional Record/Feb. 3, 1987, We Will All Be Losers, Barney Frank
Speaking Frankly*
Will The Gentleman Yield?**
The Literary Spy***
Boston Public Library-Harvard Book Store Cafe/Feb. 23, 1992, Author Series, Barney Frank
Bridgewater State College/Jan. 6, 2004, speech, Barney Frank
CSPAN 2 TV/June 25, 2004, Americans for Democratic Action speech
PBS TV/Oct. 23, 1988, The McLaughlin Group
NBC TV/Meet the Press/television transcripts

CNN TV/Crossfire/Aug. 8, 1986/July 28, 1987/Mar. 30, 1988/Jan. 20, 1989
        /Larry King Show, Oct. 14, 1998
        /Capitol Gang, Feb. 2, 2002
MSNBC TV/Mar. 3, 2004, interview, The Issue of Gay Marriage
        /Nov. 19, 1998, interview
        /July 19, 2004, Deborah Norville Show
WLVI TV/Dec. 15, 1991, 'Talking Politics'
WBPX TV/Mar. 8, 1992, interview
        /May 1995, interview with Gail Harris
NECN TV/Jan. 5, 2003, Newsnight
        /Oct. 15, 2004, Newsnight
        /Oct. 25, 2004, Newsnight
WITS/Radio transcripts
WRKO Radio Show/Apr. 24, 1987, Jerry Williams show
        /June 18, 1987, interview
        /May 21, 1992, Clapprood-Whitley show
        /April 1, 1995, News item
WBZ Radio show/July 2, 1987, David Brudnoy Show
        /June 11,1991, Steve Martorano Show

* *Times Books (c) 1992*
** *Ten Speed Press (c) 1987*
****Yale University Press (c) 2004*

About the Author

Peter Bollen is a freelance writer and former labor journalist. His work has included editing the Northeast News Service, an award-winning labor journal. He has authored several books including, Nuclear Voices, Great Labor Quotations: Sourcebook and Reader and Dear Bureaucrat. Bollen is a native of Lynn, Massachusetts and presently resides in Maine with his wife, Ellen and their cat, Harry Sneakers.

Author Index

978-0-595-38117-3
0-595-38117-0

Printed in the United States
60075LVS00006B/78